A Commentary on
1 & 2 PETER

UNLOCKING THE NEW TESTAMENT

A Commentary on
1 & 2 PETER

David Pawson

Anchor Recordings

First published in Great Britain in 2017 by
Anchor Recordings Ltd
DPTT, Synegis House, 21 Crockhamwell Road,
Woodley, Reading RG5 3LE

**For more of David Pawson's teaching,
including DVDs and CDs, go to
www.davidpawson.com**

**FOR FREE DOWNLOADS
www.davidpawson.org**

**For further information, email
info@davidpawsonministry.org**

ISBN 978-1-909886-79-7

Printed by Lightning Source

Contents

This book is based on a series of talks. Originating as it does from the spoken word, its style will be found by many readers to be somewhat different from my usual written style. It is hoped that this will not detract from the substance of the biblical teaching found here.

As always, I ask the reader to compare everything I say or write with what is written in the Bible and, if at any point a conflict is found, always to rely upon the clear teaching of scripture.

David Pawson

1

INTRODUCTION

Read 1 Peter 1:1–9

A. HIS ADDRESS (1–2)
    1. Sender (1a)
      a. Simon (Hebrew = reed); b. Petros (Greek = rock)
    2. Recipients (1b–2a)
      a. Selected by Father; b. Sanctified by Spirit
      c. Sprinkled by Son
    3. Greeting (2b)
      a. Grace; b. Peace

B. THEIR ADVANTAGES (3–8)
    1. New dimension – a living *hope* (3–5)
      a. Basis: Resurrection of Christ in past
      b. Blessing
          i. Inheritance; ii. Incorruptible
      c. Benefit
          i. It is kept for you; ii. You are kept for it.
    2. New difficulty – a tested *faith* (6–7)
      a. Basis: return of Christ in future
      b. Blessing
          i. Refined by fire; Ratified in future
      c. Benefit
          i. Courage in present; ii. Confidence in future
    3. New devotion – a joyful *love* (8–9)
      a. Basis: reality of Christ in present
      b. Blessing
          i. Invisible Jesus; ii. Inexpressible joy
      c. Benefit
          i. Scoring goal; ii. Saving grace

In the year 1666 a baker's oven set fire to the bakery and started the largest fire that London has ever seen. In the City of London there is a pillar marking the spot, now called "The Monument" with a flaming ball of fire represented on the top, and the height of that structure is the exact distance of the base from the bakery in Pudding Lane where it all began. It raged from 2nd to 6th September. Four hundred streets and thirteen thousand houses were completely destroyed. Ten million pounds' worth of damage was done. Two hundred thousand people were left homeless. St. Paul's and eighty-nine other churches were completely destroyed (Sir Christopher Wren was commissioned to rebuild most of them). Four hundred and thirty-six acres of the city, which was most of it then, was left a charred, smouldering ruin. It was not very long before rumours began, blaming people for this fire. The favourite culprits in public opinion were the French Catholics, who at that time were hated. Even Samuel Pepys in his diary claims that a French Catholic confessed to the crime of setting London ablaze. It was simply a baker's oven but when a disaster strikes there is usually a scapegoat found.

Now let us go back in imagination to 19th July AD 64. On that very day another fire started in another city – the city of Rome. Because Rome was then built largely of wooden houses and narrow streets, it spread, and for around four days it raged uncontrollably. Finally they brought it under control and then it broke out again a day or so later and raged on for another ten days. The emperor Nero watched it from the safety of his balcony and he loved it. Indeed, he said something like this: "Look at those lovely flames. They are as charming as flowers."

He was a man with great ambitions to rebuild the city of Rome. Undoubtedly, he saw in the fire his opportunity to re-plan his capital. But public opinion began to get busy. When they heard of his enjoyment of the flames they began to say that Nero had started it himself so that he could follow his building plans. So Nero found himself very unpopular. Looking around for a scapegoat, someone he could blame for starting this fire, he noticed a group of people called "Christians".

A Roman historian, Tacitus, writes this account: "Neither human assistance in the shape of imperial gifts – that is to the homeless – nor attempts to appease the gods by offering sacrifice, could remove the sinister report that the fire was due to Nero's own orders. So in the hope of dissipating the rumours, he falsely diverted the charge onto a set of people to whom the vulgar gave the name of 'Christians', and who were detested for the abominations they perpetrated. The founder of this sect, Jesus Christus by name, had been executed by Pontius Pilate in the reign of Tiberius, and the dangerous superstition, though put down for the moment, broke out again not only in Judea ... but even in Rome, where everything shameful and horrible collects and is practised."

What were the abominations of which the popular opinion accused the Christians? They were accused of cannibalism, for people heard that they ate someone's body and drank someone's blood whenever they met, and that made a good headline: "Cannibals have come to Rome." It was said they held love feasts and they saluted one another with kisses, so they were accused of foul and immoral orgies. They were also accused of preaching that the world was to be dissolved in fire, and surely they were trying to prove what they preached by setting Rome on fire.

For these abominations Nero ordered the Christians to be arrested. At first he simply crucified them as a fitting punishment for those who followed a crucified criminal. Then his sadism came out in a worse direction and he began to do other terrible things. He would dress them in the skins of wild beasts and set his hunting dogs on them. Finally, he held a garden party in the imperial palace, and to light the dark night he rolled Christians in pitch and lit them as living torches to light his garden party.

So horrible were the things he did to the Christians that public opinion revolted against Nero and they realised for the first time what a terrible emperor they had. But a "fire" of persecution, which broke out around the middle sixties in the first century AD, was going to begin a persecution of the church which would last for 250 years. Thousands would die, yet during that quarter of a millennium the church grew more strongly and more quickly than it ever grew for another fifteen hundred years.

This is the situation out of which there came a letter from Peter, who almost certainly perished in that first outbreak of persecution in Rome. All the traditions we have point that way, and indicate that Peter, the big fisherman, paid for his faith with his life. But Peter's great big heart was beating in sympathy and concern for those to whom he had preached the gospel of Jesus Christ on the day of Pentecost. For on the day of Pentecost there were people from all over the world in Jerusalem. There were people from Pontus, Cappadocia, Asia, Bithynia, and Peter realised that the persecution started by Nero would spread out like ripples to the furthermost shores of the empire and that he must prepare Christians for suffering. His heart went out towards those whom he had led to the Lord.

Peter was the kind of man who did not just lead someone to the Lord but followed it through, even years later, to help them through their problems. He wrote his first letter from Rome to Pontus, Cappadocia, Asia, and Bithynia, to his own converts to get them ready for suffering. This is the atmosphere and the theme of this little letter.

This letter prepares us for suffering. I believe that just as the Holy Spirit is breathing in a fresh way the world around and quickening his people, so Satan is doing the same to *his* people. There is coming an increasing confrontation between the forces of light and the forces of darkness, in which Christians are going to suffer more and more. Whether or not we suffer physically in Britain, we will certainly suffer socially.

Peter writes to strengthen Christians and to get them right in their relationships. We learn that a strong Christian life consists of right relationships: with Jesus (that is the subject of the first chapter); with the church (that is the subject of the second); with the emperor (even if it is a Nero); with local authorities, with your employer, with your husband or wife. As we go through the first letter, we shall see how we can get relationships right, so that when the trials come our faith is refined like pure gold.

We begin with the address. Sensibly, in those days, instead of putting the name of the person to whom the letter was going at the top of the letter and then the name of the person who sent it right at the end, they simply put at the head of the letter the address, the name of the person who was writing it, and then the name of the person who was receiving it. You might think that would say nothing to us. An address, name of the writer, name of the reader – why bother with that? It is part of the Word of God and we are going to see that the very address on the letter is full of exciting evidence of what God can do with people.

First of all, let us look at the author, the big fisherman. Fishermen tend to have strong hands because of the hard work they did. Peter had a big heart, but he was a bit unreliable and he was not very educated; an impulsive chap who would run off at a tangent. A man who, by nature, if he really found himself in a crisis would turn tail and run. Look what he says about himself.

First of all, look at his name. His parents didn't give him that name. When they got their little boy they said, "Let's call him Simon" – which means a reed, easily blown in the wind. They weren't far out in that name. The second name Simon got was from Jesus, and in the language of Aramaic, which was a kind of hybrid Hebrew mixed with a bit of Greek, Jesus said, "I'm going to call you Cephas," which means a rock – from a reed to a rock; from an unreliable person to someone who is as steady and as reliable as you can find. That is what Jesus does to people. But even that is not the name he uses here. He doesn't write, "A letter from Simon", nor "A letter from Cephas", but: "A letter from Petros". That is the Greek which we render in English "Peter". Here is an amazing miracle. When Simon first met Jesus he would not go into the house of a person who wasn't a Jew. He wouldn't sit down and have a meal with a person who wasn't a Jew, and here he is using a Greek name of himself. Here is a man who has changed his whole outlook – from having been an exclusive man who withdrew from people to a man who could invite others to call him by the Greek name that they liked to use.

Look at the place from which he is writing. He says at the end of the letter, "Those who are in Babylon salute you." Now there are two places called Babylon. One was Babel, the old capital of the kingdom of Nebuchadnezzar, but that had been lying in ruins centuries before this was written. There is a little frontier post on the Nile, which is called Babylon, but I am quite sure that is not where it was – a tiny little place and nobody there. But Babylon became the Christian nickname for a central totalitarian state capital. The same name is in the book of Revelation too. For "Babylon" stands for man's pride and power – deifying himself against God. There was one place that was doing that in Peter's day in the year AD 64, and it was Rome. There can be no doubt Peter is writing from Rome.

What is a Palestinian fisherman doing in Rome? He is not the first person who, when he came to Christ, has found that Christ said, "Away from your home. Go somewhere you would never normally choose to live, but go there for me." Here is a Palestinian Jew giving himself a Gentile name, saying, "I'm living in a Gentile capital city", and then he gives himself a Gentile title: "apostle". Now it is a word that has very interesting meanings. In the Hebrew it means someone *sent*, a royal representative, and that is undoubtedly its basic meaning. Later, in the Latin it became the word *mitto*, *mettere* or missionary, a sent one. But in the Greek the word refers to someone who has been sent on a naval or military expedition to conquer territory for his emperor. Peter uses a title here which would be understood in that sense. Here is a fisherman claiming to be a conqueror, claiming to come and capture territory for his Lord and Master and King.

Now here is the first miracle I see in the address. When a Palestinian Jew calls himself by a Gentile name, goes to live in a Gentile city, and gives himself a Gentile title, a miracle has taken place. Has that miracle taken place in your life? – a miracle that has thrust you right out of the set in which you were born, right out of the social limitations of that little group that you belong to by nature – and enabled you to go and be all things to all men? Only the grace of Christ can turn a Simon into a Peter and send him out to do this.

Now let us look at the people to whom he is writing. Who are they? They are ordinary people. They include husbands, wives, slaves, employees, citizens of the Roman

Empire, and yet he calls them something extraordinary. He takes Jewish titles and applies them to Gentiles. Here is an incredible reversal. Here is a Jew giving himself Gentile titles writing to Gentiles and giving them Jewish titles. The whole world is getting topsy-turvy in Jesus Christ. What a cross-fertilisation there is! One of the most moving things I heard was an Israeli Jew and an Egyptian Arab praying for each other and loving each other in Christ. That is what Jesus does when he gets hold of people, turns them socially inside out and relates them to people to whom they would never have spoken.

What does Peter call the Gentiles here? "You are exiles in the dispersion." That is a phrase which Jews had used for five hundred years and more. They used it of Jewish compatriots who had been forcibly taken away into far countries, or had travelled on business and settled elsewhere. The Jews today still speak of the "Diaspora", the dispersion – the Jews scattered over the face of the earth. Their home is Israel but they live everywhere. Some of them can't get back. They are the exiles of the dispersion. Every Jew talked about the exiles, but here Peter is saying that these Christians are the real exiles. They are far from home even if they live at home.

What does that mean? It means that every Christian is a social misfit. Every Christian must come to terms with the fact that every Jew must discover: that they don't fit, that there is something different deep within them that just won't fit into the world in which we live. You may stay in the same house in which you lived before you were a Christian. You may go on living in the same town, yet somehow you don't belong anymore.

Listen to this amazing description of the early Christians I came across in a letter written by a man called Diognetus. He wrote:

"Christians are not marked out from the rest of mankind by their country, or their speech, or their customs. They dwell in cities both Greek and barbarian, each as his lot is cast, following the customs of that region in clothing and food and in the outward things of life generally. Yet they manifest the wonderful and openly paradoxical character of their own state. They inhabit the land of their birth but as temporary residents thereof. They take their share of all responsibilities as citizens and endure all disabilities as aliens. Every foreign land is their native land and every native land a foreign land. They pass their days upon earth but their citizenship is in heaven."

Do you see how Jew and Gentile in Christ become one? The deepest wall of partition has been taken away in Christ. This feeling of being different, being exiles, is something that Jew and Gentile now hold in common.

How did they get that way? What makes us Christians different from other people? Three things: we have been *selected* by God, we have been *sanctified* by the Spirit, and we have been *sprinkled* by Jesus. Those are the three dimensions of Christian difference. Peter is saying this is what makes you exiles; this is what has cut you off from the human race and made you different.

First of all, you have been *chosen* by God. That is why the Jews felt different, and we share this with Israel. If ever I have an open discussion with students and say, "You can ask any question," more often than not somebody mentions predestination. It is the loveliest truth in the Bible to the Christian, even lovelier than to the Jew. To think that God decided to have me! Why? There is nothing in me that should make him want me. Now of course, you don't realise that at the beginning of your Christian life. In September 1947, when I chose Christ, I thought I had made the decision. I thought it was all my initiative; that I was coming to him. Now I know that my decision was simply a response to his leading. The way he influenced my life in so many ways beforehand – he was choosing me. Let every Christian thank God that he was predestined to glory, that the decision was his heavenly Father's. God is a Father who decides to have children. There are no unwanted children in his family. He says, "I want you and you and you."

The tragedy is that those who are not yet Christians seize hold of this idea of predestination and they almost talk as if God should have no free will at all, and man is the only free person in the universe and God must bow to our wills. The tragedy is that they use it as an excuse for not coming to Christ. They say, "Well, he hasn't chosen me." How do they know he hasn't? If anybody says, "Well, I don't think he wants me," I say to them, "Well, you ask him. Come to him and ask him if he wants you as a child and see what he says." I've never met anybody who came to God and said, "Do you want me," and God didn't say to them, "Yes, I do. Be my child." But it was God's choice. The sense of being chosen by God is overwhelming, it doesn't make us feel any better than anybody else but it makes us feel grateful to God.

Second, how did that choice of God begin to be manifest to myself? The answer is in the Holy Spirit. Did you notice the order of these three things? Rather surprising: God, the Spirit, Jesus. Do you notice when you first become a Christian you think it is Jesus first, but it isn't. In reality: God first, second the Spirit, then Jesus. The Spirit sanctified you, which means set you apart; the Spirit began to speak to you. You didn't know that God wanted you as a child and then things began to stir. Something happened. I don't know how it happened to you. I know how it happened to me, and before I trusted Jesus, the Spirit was telling me that I needed him, and I knew it. It was the Spirit who set me apart and made the choice real to me. The Spirit set me apart and I knew that God was wanting me.

Then step number three: *sprinkled by the blood of Jesus*. I have an inheritance coming to me when I die. Now normally inheritances come when someone else dies. That is the law of inheritance. Here is an inheritance you get when you die – the best inheritance of all, because whatever else you may inherit on earth you will lose it when you die and someone else will inherit it, but here is an inheritance you get when you die. "Reserved in heaven for you" – it has my name on it. Once I went off for a conference and arrived in Amsterdam around midnight. I went to the centre where the event was to be held and it was deserted and I felt so alone. I had never been in Amsterdam before and didn't know where to make for. There didn't seem to be anywhere to go and I said a little prayer. I went up to a man in a porter's uniform who was just clearing up at the back of the building. I asked, "Can you tell me somewhere to stay? Can you tell me of a hotel nearby, or anywhere I can get a bed for the night?" He said, "Try that one over there," pointing right across the flats and the gardens to a neon sign. So I went along to this hotel, went in and said, "Would you possibly have a room for the night?" They said, "What name?" I said, "Pawson," and the girl said, "Ah yes, we have reserved room number so and so for you." It was the very hotel where I was due to stay and I walked up into the most lush room I had ever seen. Billy Graham was paying for it, so it had been reserved for me. I had discovered in a city where I didn't know whether I had a room at all that there was one in my name, and I had been led to it. I was so happy just to go into that room to lie down and go to sleep. There is a room in heaven with your name on the door – an inheritance reserved for you when you die. Not only is that being kept for you but Peter says you will be kept for it. It is reserved for you and you are guarded until the day so that God keeps that for you and you for that, and one day he will bring both together at the day of salvation when finally your salvation is complete and you walk into your room in glory. There are many other things you are going to inherit there, but there is a place reserved and you are kept for that day. That is the first blessing and we bless God for that – *a living hope* that keeps us looking to the future and gives us great confidence, and it came through the resurrection of Jesus in the past.

The second great blessing that comes is the blessing of *a tested faith*. You may not count this a blessing at first, but it is one of God's great blessings. You now have a faith in God. When you have been born again, you believe in God but that faith is going to be tested. It is not an easy life being a Christian; never believe those who say that if you come to Jesus your troubles are over – it is not true. It is much truer to say that if you come to Jesus your troubles have just begun. "In the world you will have big troubles," said Jesus – much tribulation. You will go through it. If you have not had that kind of tested faith then you have missed something, because Peter is saying that faith is like gold – fire makes it purer and better. You will have a tested faith and it will go through the fire. I don't know what fires your faith has had to go through, but I know that if you have got a strong faith it is because it has been tested by trials and troubles. Sometimes you could have thrown the whole thing in and you didn't. Why? Because that little bit of faith that was still there hung on and God with his great big hand hung on to you. Your faith held on. How precious faith is – better than gold.

When you are born again, your sense of values changes: you go through a kind of traumatic experience in which suddenly things take on a different value and the thing that becomes really precious to you is the gold of your faith – not money, but a faith that is strong. You may have thought that money can see you through every trial, but it is faith that will see you through. Therefore, you are glad when your faith is tested and it comes out purer and stronger.

Peter teaches that if you go through this kind of trouble, it will bring you praise and glory and honour in the day when Jesus returns. He will be glad you stuck it, went through with it and hung on to this faith. Do you want that praise, and glory, and honour when Jesus comes back again? You can have it. Faith more precious than gold is something that you can take with you when you go; you will leave every bit of gold you have behind, but you can take your faith with you. When Jesus comes, he will say: "Well done, you hung on through the trouble. You kept your faith and it is a stronger faith than ever." That is the second thing you can bless God for, and your faith only hangs on because of the return of Jesus in the future. As your hope is built on the resurrection of Jesus in the past, your faith hangs on to the return of Jesus in the future.

There is something even more. There is the new dimension of a living hope based on the resurrection of Jesus in the past, the new difficulty of a tested faith based on the return of Jesus in the future, and the new devotion of *a joyful love* which is based on the relationship you have with Jesus *in the present*. Jesus is not just past and future; Jesus is now – here and now. I remember a mother saying to me something like this: "You know, I've been trying for years to get my son to dress properly, brush his hair and wash his face. Suddenly, he comes home with his hair all neat, his clothes all straight, looking nice and clean and shiny. Some little fifteen-year old girl has achieved in just one week what I have failed to achieve in years!" But there was a new devotion there. Psychologists talk about "the expulsive power of a new affection". Falling in love does change you quite radically – there is a new spring of affection within you. This is the third great blessing that has come to you, and it has come from someone you have never seen.

Think of all that he has done for you – and you know what kind of person he is. You know the name of Jesus. You can talk to him and you can thank him, and you can learn to love him, but one day you will see him. You have not seen him now but you trust him, and because you trust someone you have never seen, you know the blessedness that Thomas did not know. Jesus said, "Blessed are those who have not seen yet have trusted." The blessedness is of a sheer, joyful, happy love. There is nothing so wonderful as being happy and loving Jesus.

A verger was walking around a cathedral one day and he saw a woman standing in front of a picture of the crucifix showing Jesus on the cross. She was muttering to herself, and the verger wondered if she was a little unusual and whether he should ask her to leave, or whether she wanted help. So he edged close to her to hear what she was saying. Staring at the picture, she was just saying, "Oh, how I love him" – that's all.

That is a dimension and a love that will never be broken; a love that will never have to say goodbye; a love that you will never lose. "Blessed be the God and Father of our Lord Jesus Christ." His resurrection in the past has given us a living hope. His return in the future enables us to hang on to our faith even when it is tough. His relationship with us in the present fills us with a love that you just cannot put into words – it is too happy. What is the result of all this? The result is the salvation of your soul.

What is salvation? It is exactly the same as the word "salvage". During World War 2 we salvaged everything we could – paper, scrap iron. I remember the day that our front gate went away for salvage. We salvaged everything we could. Things that nowadays in our affluent society we throw out and pollute our rivers with, things that we throw out as useless and say we're finished with, no use to us at all, during the war we salvaged things like that. We made them useful. We made them serve a purpose; they were needed.

When God looked down at the world he could have said, "Oh, I wash my hands of such a mess. I can't do anything with it." Martin Luther once said, "If I were God I'd have kicked the whole world to pieces long ago." But when God looked down, he said, "I'm going to salvage those people – those useless people, those people who can't do anything for anybody else, those people whom I made to serve me; they just can't serve me, they are no good at it. I'm going to salvage them; I am going to give them a new hope, a new faith, and a new love and I will make them useful. I can use them because I want them." That is salvation and God is doing this the world over. He will salvage thousands of people this very day, and from being useless people they will become useful to God in his service. He can do it for you if you will only let him.

2

SANCTIFICATION

Read 1 Peter 1:10–22

A. MESSENGERS OF GOD – revelation (10–12)
    1. Earthly – prophets (10–12a)
      a. Crucifixion
      b. Exaltation
    2. Heavenly – angels (12b)
      a. Longing; b. Looking

B. MARKS OF GODLINESS – response (13–22)
    1. Conviction (13)
      a. Active mind; b. Stable hope
    2. Obedience (14)
      a. Old – what I want; b. New – what he wants
    3. Holiness (15–16)
      a. You be holy; b. I am holy
    4. Fear (17)
      a. Impartial judgement; b. Reverent anxiety
    5. Gratitude (18–20)
      a. Not money but blood
      b. Chosen then, revealed now
    6. Confidence (21)
      a. Present faith
      b. Future hope
    7. Love (22)
      a. Brotherly
      b. Sincere

This passage is about the privileges and the responsibilities of being a Christian. One definition of a privilege is to have something that others don't have and would love to have if they could. We have enough food and others don't have that. It is a privilege to have a meal. I think we would be less fussy with our food and less fond of it if we recognised and remembered that other people would give anything for the crumbs under our table. Likewise, it is a spiritual privilege to be a Christian and to have been brought up in a land that has had so much opportunity. When I consider the blessings that England has had, I am amazed that God is still patient with us. Think of the privileges we have had – to have had the gospel for nearly two thousand years. We have had it almost as long as Greece. Roman soldiers first brought Christianity to our shores. We have had so many Bibles in English, more than any other language in the world.

But the privilege that Peter mentions here, seeking to increase in his readers a sense of deep gratitude to God, concerns two groups of intelligent beings who would love to have seen Christ and would love to have experienced his salvation but didn't. They are two groups whom you never think about until you become a Christian: the prophets and the angels – some human beings and some supernatural beings. Both these two groups knew about Christ, but neither group knew what we know.

Take the prophets: a mighty army of men all down through the centuries before Jesus. Here are some of their names: Enoch, Abraham, Isaac, Jacob, Moses, Elijah, Elisha, Isaiah, Jeremiah, Ezekiel, Daniel, Hosea, Amos, and so you could go on. These men were like blind lamplighters. This was their role – to go through a dark world and to strike a little light, yet at the time they themselves did not understand what the light meant. They actually presented to us, in bits and pieces, the entire story of Jesus and yet each one presented just a little piece.

It is great fun to do a jigsaw, but you start with little odd pieces. You recognise just a little bit here and a little bit there, "that's a flower" and, "that's a human face" – you begin to put them together but you and I go by the picture on the box. The real enthusiast doesn't have a picture on the box and it takes them weeks to get it put together. But we cheat; we have got the whole picture, so we say, "Ah, that goes there," and we begin to place the pieces.

The prophets were each given a piece of the jigsaw and they faithfully told people what was on the face of the piece. They caught a vision of Jesus, but just a tiny little fragment. One knew that he was going to be born of a virgin. Another knew that he would have to flee into Egypt. Another knew that he would be anointed with the Holy Spirit. Another knew that he would be betrayed by one of his own friends. Another knew that he would be given vinegar to drink on a cross. Another knew that his hands and feet would be pierced. Another knew that he would be buried in a rich man's grave. Another knew that he would be raised on the third day, but each one just knew a little piece. As they looked at that piece, they said, "Who is that? When is he going to come?"

The prophets searched and inquired into the very things they had spoken about. They did not understand. Often at the cost of their own lives and certainly at the cost of their position and popularity, they spoke faithfully about the little piece they had. One thinks of Russian Christians in the communist era, who only had one page of the Bible and they would talk about it.

We have been given the whole truth of Jesus. "God, who in

the olden times, spoke to our fathers through the prophets," says the letter to the Hebrews, "... has now spoken to us in his Son." We have got the lid of the box. We can see where all those prophets' bits and pieces fit in. What a privilege to live in A.D., not B.C. Thank God you are living today. Even though it is a horrible world to live in, thank God you were born after Jesus. The prophets said: "Who is it? When will he come?" They did not even know the most precious name of Jesus.

The other group that Peter mentions is the angels. Here again was a group that do not know what I know about Jesus. They had known him as the Son of God. They had looked up to him, they had worshipped him, and they had served him (for more about them see my book *Angels*). Above man in the order of creation is a wonderful order of intelligent beings, superior to us in strength, intelligence, in speed and beauty called angels. They are real. There are myriads of them and one day you will see them if you know Jesus. One day they looked down and they saw the Son of God in the form of a little baby. They worshipped and said, "Glory to God." But the angels never know Jesus as we do. What don't the angels know about him? They never know him as Saviour. They never know him as the one who takes away sin. They can't know him as that because when Jesus died on a cross, the Bible says he died not for angels, but for men and women. Because of the cross, men and women are going to be lifted above the angels. What a privilege that even the angels in heaven don't know what I know of his love and of his mercy, though they worship him as king.

So here is the great thing that Peter says to be thankful for. You were born in the right time and in the right place. You were created on earth in the Anno Domini era, in the days of our Lord. Therefore, count your blessings; count it a holy privilege that you can shout aloud the name of

Jesus today. But privileges bring responsibilities. One of the deep principles of the Bible is that if you have been given a privilege by God, he will call you to account for the responsible use of it.

In the rest of this passage there are seven responsibilities. They are not very exciting or glamorous and there is nothing popular about them, but these are things that God expects from you for the privilege of knowing Jesus as Saviour. Here is the first one: he expects you to *have conviction*. Conviction is: to "gird up the loins" of your mind; to love God with all your intelligence; to use what thought powers he has given you, and to know and be ready to talk to other people about him. That phrase "gird up the loins" of your mind sounds a bit archaic, so: roll up the sleeves of your mind; tighten the belt of your mind. There was an Irish building labourer I knew of who, whenever he was going to lift a bag of cement, would take his belt up a hole or two. Having belted himself, he then lifted the weight. Peter is teaching that the first responsibility you have – since you have the picture on the box lid, since you have got the whole of Christ, since you know him as Saviour – is to *think straight*. To gird up the loins of your mind, to know what you believe, to be able to talk to someone about what you believe, to *think about Jesus in the right way*.

That involves being sober. This not only refers to alcohol, but it certainly includes that. A man who is drunk can't think straight. He will say things that are not rational and meaningful. So we are to be sober that way, but the phrase means something more: don't get intoxicated with new ideas, with fashions of thinking, with crazes and with ideologies that come and go. Don't get brainwashed by the mass media. We live in a day of entertainment; when people are picking up their ideas from media. Ideas are being fed out to the multitude, but God expects you as a Christian, to be a person who thinks for yourself, not afraid to think differently from everybody else. You need to be able to say, "I have thought it through and what you are saying to me is a pack of lies. It's not true; I know the truth." Gird up the loins of your mind and be sober. Don't get tossed around with the latest ideas; don't adopt the latest opinions.

What then should you do? To keep sober, you need an *anchor*. You need something that will keep your mind fixed as a compass is fixed to the North Pole or the magnetic pole, wherever it has moved. What is your mind to be fixed on to think straight? "Set your hope on the grace that will be revealed at the coming of the Lord Jesus." If you keep your mind fixed on that, then you won't be tossed about; you won't adopt the latest crazes. You will say, "There's one thing I know that's true: Jesus is coming back." That is the key for sober thinking in the Christian life, to realise that Jesus is on his way back to earth. You will then think straight about everything else.

Some of the things that people think are so important cease to be important because Jesus is coming back. Some of the things which people ignore become desperately important because Jesus is coming back. When you hear politicians promising some great era on earth that they can bring in, you say, "I don't believe it; Jesus is coming back. I know where my hope is fixed. Therefore, I can think straight about politics, about education, about science, about all the movements of man. I can look through them and say, 'Jesus is coming back.'"

The second responsibility of those who have the privilege of knowing Jesus is *obedience*. To be converted is simply to change bosses. The freedom that we have is not a freedom to boss ourselves; we never had that and we never can have that. Every human being is made to obey someone or something. Let me tell you what bosses you have changed – what boss you served and what Lord you serve now. Peter says there was a time when you served the passions of your ignorance. You were a slave; you thought you were free but you were a slave of the things that you wanted and you were gripped by them. A man can be possessed by his possessions. He thinks he is possessing them but they are possessing him.

There was a man once walking around his mansion and he was looking at the collection of fine, expensive paintings that he had collected. Looking at these paintings, his butler overheard him saying to them, "Oh, you make it so hard for me to die." He was possessed by his possessions; he was a slave. The Bible tells us that until you know Jesus you are a slave to yourself. That is the worst kind of slavery you can imagine. Behind the passions of your ignorance is Satan. Whether you realised it or not, you were right under his thumb and he could do what he liked with you.

When I became a Christian, did I become free to boss myself? No, I became free to obey another boss, a much better one to work for, a much more considerate one to serve and so he is now my Lord. I am called to a life of obedience, not a life in which I can now do what I want, but a life in which I can now do what *he* wants. That is the second responsibility for knowing Jesus. In God's children, as in every other child, disobedience is a disgrace to the parents as well as to the children. It is a matter of embarrassment when children are disobedient.

The third responsibility is *holiness*. Let the world deride holiness if they will. The Bible says, "Be ye holy for I am holy." Let the world call us "Holy Joes" or "Holier than thou". But let us say that God is a holy God and we want to be like Dad. I hope you don't think that is irreverent but when you are born again there is born within you a desire to be like your heavenly Father, because he is so wonderful.

What does it mean to say that God is holy? The word

"holy" means *different*. Don't follow Jesus unless you are prepared to be different from other people. There is a kind of subtle temptation to want to prove that you are just like everybody else when you are a Christian. You are not. You may try to laugh at that joke, but you can't. It becomes a kind of sick grin. To be holy is to be different, but different in what way? Not different in dress, not different in using the English language or the Greek, but different in being like Jesus, which means to be utterly straight, utterly clean, utterly pure, utterly holy. That is what the word means. "Holy" means clean, upright. The world doesn't need more clever people. The world doesn't need more rich men and women. The world doesn't deeply need more well-fed people. What it really needs is more godly people. Indeed, that I think is the loveliest description of any Christian you could ever hear. "He is a godly man," "she is a godly woman." That tells us something of what the word "holy" means.

The fourth responsibility we have is this: *to be men and women of fear*. How do you ever get holy? It is a combination of the right kind of fear and the right kind of love. Let it be the right kind of fear. Peter says that we are to *fear God* – we are to conduct ourselves with fear while we are down here, before we get to heaven. There will be no fear needed in heaven, but there is fear needed here among Christians. This fear is something that perhaps we need to recover.

In the early days of the Society of Friends, they were called Quakers because when they gathered together for meetings and God came into the meeting, they quaked. The floors on which they sat trembled, so people called them the "Quakers". They feared God and there is a place for fearing God. Don't misunderstand me here. When we do something that displeases God and we confess it, the blood of Jesus takes it away and it is forgiven and forgotten. I am referring to those things we have never put right – those things that

God wanted us to do that we never did. I am referring to the people he wanted us to talk to and we didn't talk to them for embarrassment; I am referring to the missed opportunities. There is a fear that is right and good. If we fear God in this loving way, we will never fear anyone or anything else.

The fifth thing: *gratitude*. The Christian life is not to be a life of grumbling, but a life of gratitude. I remember when Richard Wurmbrant came to our home and sat down and talked to us. I remember him telling us then that he was actually ransomed. He was bought from the communists by Christians in the West. In the communist countries they were so keen for sterling and for Western money that they began to sell prisoners to anyone who would pay for them. Of course, we asked Richard Wurmbrant, "How much did you cost?" He said, "Twelve hundred pounds."

He continued, "I shall always be grateful to the Christians who paid for my freedom." I wonder how much you would be worth. How much I would be worth? What would anybody feel like spending to set me free? What am I worth? To the scientists I might consist of a pound's worth of chemicals – of fat, of sugar, of water. Am I worth more than that? Well, every child in Britain has had some tens of thousands of pounds spent on them by their family and the State by the time they go out to work. That is what this country considers a child is worth. What an incentive to go out and do a youthful job and repay some of that to the community who has done that for you! But is that what we are worth? Let me tell you what every human being is worth to God. Not silver or gold, which get devalued or stolen and perish, but the precious blood of Jesus. There is something more precious than all the money in my pocket. It is the blood in my veins because that is my life. I could spend all the money I have on you and still keep my blood. But God looked at you and loved you, and gave the blood of his Son for you. You were redeemed, you were ransomed, you were set free – not with money, not with silver or gold, but with the blood of Jesus Christ. What were you set free from? Peter teaches that you were set free from two things. One is futility, getting nowhere. "Life," said someone, "is like a roundabout – you get on, you go round and round and round and have a great time and you get off just where you got on." That is futility. There are many people who lead a wasted life, getting nowhere fast, with just nothing to look forward to, gripped by meaninglessness and futility. If you listen to many songs today, if you read some of the trash being published, you find that they say "futility", that there is nothing, that it is meaningless and useless. The precious blood of Jesus bought you out of that.

I was talking to forty young people some years ago. I said to them, "Write down on a piece of paper the biggest blessing that Christ has brought into your life," because they had all just become Christians. Out of the forty young people, thirty-eight wrote: "Purpose; I know where I'm going. I know what life's about. My life is now meaningful." They felt that their lives were now part of a gigantic purpose of God and were being caught up into a meaningful existence. You were ransomed from futility.

The other thing Peter is saying is: you were ransomed from the futile ways inherited from your fathers. He is referring in that phrase to religious tradition that is dead. That phrase means all the religion that men think up that is passed down, that you inherit, and it is hollow and dead. When you meet Christ, you are done with religion because Christ and religion don't mix. To be set free from religion is marvellous. You are set free from that and now it is Jesus. That is different.

What is the difference between Jesus and religion? All religion is man trying to get through to God; Jesus is God coming through to man. All religion is man trying to save

35

himself; Jesus is God saving you. Do you see the difference? All that cost Jesus his blood, and cost him his very life. No wonder we are grateful. You are grateful when you ask how much did a thing cost and you are grateful if you ask how much thought was there behind it. Isn't that true? Those are the two things that make you grateful for a present.

I remember one of the presents I got as a little boy and I still have part of it. It was a little set of carpentry tools: a file and a chisel and a little saw. The chisels, the screwdriver and the file had handles made out of branches of a tree, just roughly carved and pushed onto the steel part. I suppose it would have cost a small sum in those days to put together, but the man who gave it to me was called "Pansy" – at least that was his nickname. He was a boxer well known on Tyneside and everybody backed Pansy Tate. Pansy Tate saw more of the inside of prison than the outside of it. He knew Shakespeare backwards because it was the only book they gave him in jail, but Pansy met Jesus and Pansy wanted to do something for someone and he put all the thought he could into what he could do for a child. He carved those handles and he spent his last penny on those files and that screwdriver. How much did it cost? I suppose nearly everything he had got. How much thought went into it? You could see that; he just laboured for another person.

How much did it cost God? Everything he had – his own Son and the blood of his Son. When did he think about it? How much thought went into that gift? Before the foundation of the world God was thinking about it. Do you realise that before he made this universe and flung those planets out into space, he knew that David Pawson would need a Saviour and that you would too? All the thought and the love that went into that! Doesn't that make you grateful? Aren't you full of thanks?

The sixth mark of a real Christian today is *confidence*.

Your faith and hope are to be in God. The world is packed with pessimists, people looking on the gloomy side, people saying, "I don't know what the world's coming to." A Christian should never be depressed by the world around him. He should say, "I know what the world is coming to. It is coming to Jesus one day, and every knee shall bow and every tongue confess. I know what is going to happen: the kingdom of God is going to come and God's will is going to be done on earth as it is in heaven."

A Christian may be pessimistic about mankind, aware that man will go on making a mess, wrecking the world. But God is on the throne so you are an optimist in Christ. We are people who have hope.

Peter says that your faith and hope are *in God*. But you can't mention faith and hope without something else. Have you noticed that in the Bible wherever somebody mentions faith and hope, they can't stop, because there are three lovely things in the Christian life. The final thing (v. 22) is *love* – that this should be the mark of Christians. The privilege of being a Christian carries with it the responsibility of loving one another. That is the love referred to here by Peter. The mark that the world must see in us is a love that Christ has produced in us that bridges all social distinctions. We Christians are brothers and sisters in one big family. Isn't it terrific if you meet a brother you didn't know you had? We are in the same family and we are going to live together in the same home one day. When the world can see people of different races and backgrounds being one, then they have seen the mark which is the responsibility of the true Christian.

This has been a very simple study. Underlying this passage are words like these: children, father, brothers. Have you noticed that, all the way through? If somebody asks me why God ever created people, the answer is very simple:

he wanted a bigger family. The Father had one Son, but he wanted more children. He wanted them to be brothers and sisters. That is why he sent Jesus; that is why Jesus poured out his blood – that we might live responsibly, as a family of God.

What a privilege it is to live in our time, with Jesus having come and died for us, and much nearer than many people were to his return. What a privilege, but what an awful responsibility that we should be holy, thinking, confident, God-fearing, loving people.

3

REGENERATION

Read 1 Peter 1:23–2:3

A. CONTRAST: DON'T HAVE TO DIE (1:23–25)
    1. The seed (23a)
      a. Perishable
      b. Imperishable
    2. The word (23b–25)
      a. Timely
      b. Timeless

B. COMPARISON: DO HAVE TO DEVELOP (2:1–3)
    1. (1) Keeping clean
      a. Malice
      b. Guile
      c. Insincerity
      d. Envy
      e. Slander
    2. (2–3) Keeping fed
      a. Spiritual
      b. Digestible
      c. Wholesome
      d. Nourishing
      e. Appetising

Rummaging through all the stuff one accumulates, I came across a little photograph album and a photograph of myself – in September 1947, when I was born again, "one-day old". Angels were thrilled that day. Of course, every time a baby is born, you know that there is going to be a death some day. It may come soon or late, it may come quickly or slowly. It may come easily or in a very difficult way, but you know as soon as a baby has set foot on the road of life that they are walking to the grave. So why are the angels so excited when someone gets born again? Because that day a life starts that need never die. This is why I am in the midwifery business. That is a preacher's job. In the Bible there is the power to give people life. Peter had this power within his grasp, to hand on to others. He talks about it in these few verses. He talks about life. You see, the thing that you need is not to be able to turn over a new leaf, but the thing that everybody needs is to discover a new life, because all of us have ruined the old one.

The tragedy is that, as I turn the pages of my family album, I see an innocent little baby becoming a mischievous looking boy. It doesn't look too bad in the early years, but later he is beginning to look a bit more mischievous. Then there are photographs of me with my sisters, and the looks towards them are not always terribly loving. There is a photograph of me at the age of six with my father and a friend of his, a bank manager, playing with my train – though actually they said they were just telling me how to put it together. There is a rather selfish, angry, disgruntled little boy of six in the background.

That innocent baby grew up, and so did you, and you spoiled the life that God gave you – spoiled it by learning to say "no" before you said "yes"; you spoiled it by learning to look after number one. You spoiled it by wanting to get everything you could. You spoiled it by losing your temper. You spoiled it because you learned fairly early that words can hurt. You spoiled it by learning that it was easy to be rude, that it gave you something of a thrill to say nasty things about other people. You learned to fight, sometimes with your fists and sometimes with your tongue, and you spoiled it. God isn't interested in patching up anyone's life; he is not interested in just doing a spring clean on someone. What he really wants to do is give a brand new life to people. The greater the mess you have made of the life that you got at your birth, then the greater the wonder of the news that you can have a new life.

So Peter talks about being *born again*. That is not just an expression, it is a literal description of what happens when someone becomes a Christian. What actually happened at the time that Peter was describing about meeting Jesus was not just that he got a relationship, he got a brand new life. I know that the habits of the old life tend to hang around a bit and cause embarrassment, but the proof that you have got a new life is that you now hate it when you do those silly and sinful things. There is a new life that has been born. Just as I began as a tiny cell within my mother's body, and at first it may not have been obvious to anyone that I was on the way, later it would be. So within every Christian a new life has been born that may not be too obvious at first, but will increasingly be noticed by other people. They will say, "Whatever has happened to you?"

It is this miracle of creation that is what we mean by getting converted. We don't mean joining a church; we don't mean going through a ritual rigmarole. We mean having a new life put within you, a life that is able to respond to God, because by nature you were dead to God. The life that you got when you were born was a life that centred on self, not on God. It was a life that was built around the nucleus of a capital "I". It was not built around him, but the new life is. Now the contrast between the old life that you got when you were born and the new life that you got when you were born again is that the old life must die; the new life needn't.

So Peter describes what is true of every example of life in nature – that every example of life must die. Wonderful though it is, take a little seed—the tiniest seed, the mustard seed. Have you seen a mustard seed? You almost need a magnifying glass to see it, yet in those little specks in the hollow of your hand, there is life. It is an amazing thing and out of that tiny little speck, can grow a shrub big enough for birds to come and make nests in it. The marvel of life in a seed! Yet the tragedy is that the life in that seed cannot last forever.

When a new office block was being constructed in London some years ago, the foundation, floor and some of the walls of a Roman temple were unearthed that had been buried for nearly two thousand years. It was a Roman temple of Mithras. There was the old stone altar where they worshipped the sun god. Lying on the altar were some grains of corn that had been offered as part of a kind of harvest festival to that god. They looked dead. Yet those grains were planted and after all those centuries the little bit of life that was in those small seeds grew. Yet the wheat that grew from them died.

The New Testament uses two words for seed. Sometimes it is an animal word: "sperm". Sometime it is a vegetable word: "spore". One apostle says that when you were converted, God planted his "sperm" in you. Another apostle says that, when you were converted, God planted his "spore" in you. They are just using picture language from nature to say that when you became a Christian, God put a tiny bit of life in you – that it has got to grow. It is alive. It has got to come out and it has got to show. If there is life there, it has to grow into Christian character. "Whoever is born of God cannot go on committing sin, for the sperm of God abides in him," says John.

We had a tarmac area in front of our front door with dandelions coming straight through it. You can lay a concrete path and you find that a weed can crack it. I began my ministry in the Shetland Islands where there is the oldest granite in the British Isles, which is very popular for tombstones. It had a great commercial value, but it is terribly hard. In the days before powerful machinery, do you know how they split that granite? They had a drill with an expensive bit that bored a series of little holes in the granite. Then they would go to a tree and snap off pieces of branch and drop a piece into each hole. Then they would pour water on top of the branch every day for a fortnight. After a fortnight the granite split because there was life there – the cells which God had made were alive and the granite had to give. If you have been born again, there has been planted within you a life that can bring everything else to nothing. That life will crack habits that seem so hard that you would never otherwise have got rid of them. This new life pushes other things out of the way. So Peter says that you were born anew of imperishable seed. Only God the Creator can plant something in your life that will not die. Everything else you plant in your life will go; it has got to, but not this. This is everlasting life. "The flowers fade and die," says Peter. The grass goes. All of life in nature, wonderful though it is, dies. One day, even the universe itself is to go, but the word that God plants never goes.

Now how does God plant this word? How do I receive this

seed? How does it come into my life? *That seed is planted in your heart when you hear the word of God.* That is why I am a preacher – I am a sower. Many years ago, somebody said to me, "Now that you've given up farming, you have really changed your occupation, haven't you?" I didn't! I am just planting different seeds and they are getting better crops because I know that everlasting life can come from the seeds I am now able to plant.

The seed that is planted is the word—Jesus said that. He told parables of farmers sowing seed and he said the seed is the word. It is the word that God says to you, and that word is now enshrined in a book, but if it stays within the covers of the Bible it is buried and it can't produce anything. It needs to be planted. The seed is no use until it is in the soil. This book is no use until it is in your heart. You can have a Bible at home and keep it on the shelf, but it will do nothing whatever for you until the seed is planted. That either means that you must read it for yourself or you must listen to someone else read it to you – tell you about it. But some way, what God has said has got to be planted deep in your heart. As soon as it is, then it begins to germinate and grow.

The amazing thing to me is that people can resist this word. It is so true about them. Every time you read your Bible it is like looking in a mirror. You see yourself. Yet people can listen to a sermon and go home and think no more about it. They have listened to the word of God, hearing it read out and preached to them in person, yet they can go away and forget it. Jesus talked about people like that. He said they are like rock; they are hard soil. Or else, they are shallow soil and they think about it for just a little while, but they don't think about it deeply enough, and then it goes. Worst of all, a person sits in church and listens to the word and it gets into their heart, but Satan meets them as soon as they leave the church and says, "If you let that stay there, your life is going to have to change; you are going to lose some of your friends; you're going to have to stop doing certain things." He is able to pluck it out of their heart before it can get root. But now and again someone listens to the word of God, it goes in deep and they say, "That's me. Who's told that preacher about me? How does God know that I'm like that?" The word goes in and it settles and they can't forget it. It grows, and the roots begin to get in, and life begins. Not every Christian can say it was on a particular date that life began. That does not matter as long as it has begun – as long as life has germinated and started to push up to the daylight.

It is through the seed of the word, the good news preached or the good news about Jesus. So when you have become a Christian, you have been born anew. You have started life all over again. You have literally become as a little baby. As a little child you have got to learn all over again. Sometimes new Christians feel, "Oh I shall never be a grown up Christian. I'll never be a saint. I'll never be as good as these other people around me." They were once babies too; they had to learn to talk a new language. They had to learn to address a new Father. So Peter, having described being born again, goes on to describe what is needed by a little baby. So I turn from being born again to the comparison between the two lives that you have—the physical and the spiritual, between being born and born again. The *contrast* is that your physical life has to die, but your spiritual life can live forever. The *comparison*, in which they are alike, is that your physical life and your spiritual life both need care. I remember when my wife and I came away from the maternity home with our little baby, and the sister's very practical advice to us was: "Keep one end full and the other end empty and you won't go far wrong." We came away with our little baby with these two simple rules. It is those two rules that Peter takes up in the first three verses of chapter two. Someone who has been born again needs washing and feeding. They need to be kept clean and they need to be kept fed. It is as simple as that. What is that first thing that you do when a baby is born into the world, after they have cried their first cry and breathed their first breath? You wash them – you clean them up and you take away from them all the traces of their former existence. Isn't that the first thing to do? With a spiritual baby it is the same. You will never grow up and be a healthy Christian unless you get washed clean of the dirt from your former existence before you were born again.

I existed for nine months before I was born. I don't take my birthday back to the day of my conception (though the Japanese do) but I take it back to the day I was born. Similarly, I take my Christian life back to the day I was born again, but I existed before that and I must be washed clean of that which clings from my existence before. What is the kind of dirt that clings to a Christian, of which a new baby Christian needs to be cleansed? Here are some things that can go on clinging and become a source of dangerous ill health to the Christian, so that growth is thwarted and stunted.

Number one: *malice*. The kind of life you lived before you were a Christian had malice in it. It is a perverted joy in hurting someone else, giving as good as you get, taking your revenge. If someone did that to you, then you did it to them. If they don't speak to you, alright you'll cut them dead—that's malice. It is part of the dirt that has got to be washed off if we are going to be healthy babies and grow up. No more malice; no more resentment to that person who did that. No more resentment to that awkward boss. Malice is gone and there is no desire to bring a person down a peg or two.

The second thing that can cling to a newborn spiritual baby is *guile*, being deceitful. According to the Bible, the heart is deceitful. You learn this with children so quickly.

Even as children we learn that you can cover up something wrong by telling a lie. That is something that has got to be washed away when you are born again. You have got to be finished with deceiving people and trying to manipulate them. When Jesus met a man called Nathanael he said, "Look, behold a true Israelite in whom is no guile." What a compliment! A true Christian is to be someone of whom others can say, "There is a true Christian who is no snake in the grass, someone in whom there is no guile, no underhand method – an open, honest, upright person."

Thirdly, *insincerity* – if there is one thing that has no place in the Christian life it is hypocrisy. One thing Jesus hated was play-acting, people not being themselves; people putting on a veneer, hiding behind an exterior. Jesus wanted honesty, even if that honesty revealed things that were not very nice; he would much rather have that, openness and honesty. Insincerity is something that needs to be washed off a newborn spiritual babe.

Fourthly, *envy*, which is a horrible thing. It was responsible for the first murder in history and the worst murder in history. Envy is that cancer that eats out a person who looks at another and says, "They've got more opportunities than I have; they've got more money than I have. They've got more gifts than I have; they've got more friends than I have," and begins to be full of self-pity. Envy is a horrible thing. Alas, it works even among Christians. You can envy a fellow believer's experience, yet it is part of our former life.

Fifthly and finally: *slander*. I would rate gossip far higher in my priority of sins than almost anything else. Slander is the devil's own work. The philosopher Pascal said, "If everyone knew what each had said of the other, there would not be four friends left in the world." You gossiped before you were born again. Everybody talks about people – not just the ladies, the men do too. Gossip is a dreadful thing, but when you become a newborn babe in Christ it is one of the things that has got to be washed away – for health. Here then are five things which are not crude, obvious sins; they are all very subtle. It goes without saying that sins like murder, adultery and stealing are to be left behind when you are born again, but we don't always realise that things like gossip, malice and envy are to be washed away if you are going to grow up.

So on the negative side a new baby needs to be cleaned, and on the positive side is a need to be fed ("to keep the other end full") and to feed the baby with something that will help it to grow. You will never grow as a Christian unless you feed this life within you. With what kind of food? Peter says: "as newborn babes, long for the milk". The word he uses in the Greek language is "lunge" for the milk. Have you ever watched a baby suckling at the mother's breast? A baby keen to get breakfast lunges, eager to get the milk. Peter is saying: as newborn spiritual babies, lunge at your nourishment; want it more than anything else.

You need nourishment that has five characteristics. First, it must be *spiritual*. As your physical life is fed with physical food, your spiritual life is fed with spiritual food. It is food for the soul. The one thing that is food for the soul is the very same thing that was the cause of the seed of life being implanted in your life: the word of God. The spiritual food we need is to be found in the Bible. Nobody ever grew up to be a mature, healthy Christian who did not read and read it. I know it is not an easy book. You could start with Luke's Gospel, and read that through, then Acts, then the letter of James. Feed on it. Take it with you to work and read it in a little gap after lunch, but feed on it until you begin to grow.

Second: you need *digestible* food. Some parts of the Bible are very meaty and you have to chew and chew, but some are milk. Psalm 23 is milk. You can read that straightaway as a newborn babe and you can suck it in and nourish your soul on it. So be sensible in this. Don't try to eat what you are not ready for. Don't worry if certain things the preacher says seem to go right over your head. There will come a day when you will understand all that is preached, but don't worry as long as you have got something. I don't expect people to remember everything I have said in a sermon. You have an amazing memory if you do – I can't remember everything I have said myself. Sometimes I am very surprised when someone quotes me and I can't remember saying that at all. I wonder whether they thought I said it or whether I really did!

If you, a listener, take one simple thought from a sermon of mine, then it has been worth preaching. The funny thing is that you find one person takes one thought and another takes another and so on. So I pour out a lot of thoughts in one sermon and hope that those who are newborn babes will get a little milk at some point. Some will be able to chew the deeper bits and get the meat, but don't worry if you can't eat it all at first. Long for the milk, the meat can come along later. I try to put a bit of gravy on it and make it a little attractive, but even so there will come a time when you can get your teeth into it. Jeremiah says, "I have eaten your word" – I have digested it, taken it right in.

Third, the food you need is *pure*. The milk must be sterilised. Alas, the tragedy is that we live in a world in which people have taken the pure word of God and mixed it with their own ideas and their own philosophies and cut bits out and put in their own words in place. That is happening all the time. You mustn't mix your intake with man's ideas. It must be the unadulterated word of God. If somebody tells you something that you can't find in the Bible, don't eat it; don't drink it, don't take it in.

Fourth, spiritual food must be *nourishing*. Milk contains all kinds of things. On the farm I used to enjoy what was called "beasting pudding". I wonder if you know what that is. It is made from the third milking after a cow has calved. It is a special kind of milk and you can make it into a delicious custard and it is awfully good for you, because in the early milk of a cow there are all sorts of extra nutrients which get a calf going and the milk provides antibodies. You need that nourishing kind of milk that has everything in it that will help you to be protected against the attacks, the invasion, the infection of evil which is going to be all around you.

Finally, it is *appetising*. There is something wrong if a newborn Christian baby finds the word of God boring. If you start feeding on spiritual food, it is something that you find appetising. You taste the kindness of the Lord. What you taste is good, and you want more. If you are a young Christian and are not finding the food appetising, then you must be on the wrong kind of food. You must have failed to taste the kindness of the Lord, for as you feed on the word of God you begin to say, "Isn't the Lord kind? Isn't he good to me?" The Lord is kind to a little baby, helping and protecting.

We have been thinking about only six verses. What a little gem this passage is. Peter is talking about being born again into a new life, then he goes on to say what that new life needs. It needs washing clean and it needs nourishing. If you don't go on from that new birth to be washed and to be fed, then don't blame God if your Christianity doesn't taste good. Don't blame him if you don't grow up as others grow up.

My last word on this passage must be this: have you been born again? You could have the *outside* of a Christian, but not have the *inside*. You could go to church; you could behave like other Christians. But in the last analysis, unless you have been born again, you are going to die forever. So I ask you: have you received the word of God about Jesus into your heart? Do you believe it to be true that Jesus the Son of God came to this earth to die in your place, to pay for your sins, and rose again that his Holy Spirit might live in your life and make it new? Do you believe that? Have you taken it in? Then, if so, you have been born again. The new life has begun. But if you haven't, then God help you, for no-one else can.

4

ADAPTATION

Read 1 Peter 2:4–17

A. TO GOD (4–10)

    1. A NEW TEMPLE (4–8)
      a. Christ – living stone
          i. Erected by God; ii. Rejected by men
      b. Christians – living stones
          i. Spiritual house; ii. Holy priesthood;
          iii. acceptable sacrifices

    2. A NEW PEOPLE (9–10)
      a. Once you were
          i. Not a people; ii. Not received mercy
      b. Now you are
          i. Chosen people; ii. Royal priesthood;
          iii. Holy Nation

B. TO WORLD (11–17)

    1. SUSPECTED ALIENS (11–12)
      a. Accused – bad doings
      b. Absolved – good deeds
          i. Visible; ii. Vindicated

    2. OBEDIENT CITIZENS (13–14)
      a. King – supreme
      b. Governors – sent
          i. Chastise wrong; ii. Command right

    3. FREE MEN (15–16)
      a. Not diplomatic immunity
      b. But divine integrity
          i. Respect all; ii. God; iii. King

Sometimes we make the mistake of saying, "Come to me" and sometimes churches say, "Come to us." But true Christianity says, "Come to him", and that is how it all begins. But the verb here translated "come" ought to be put into English as: "Keep on coming to him." It is not just come *once*. Come to Jesus is the secret of growing in the Christian life. One day he is coming to us and coming to take us.

But to whom? Who is Jesus and what is he? In the pages of the Bible, two hundred and fifty names and titles are given to him. Here we are going to concentrate only on Jesus the "rock" or "cornerstone".

After the Six Day War in Israel I visited a village in a northern region of the country that I had often heard about but never seen. In Old Testament times it was called Dan. Later it was called Paneas, after the god Pan. Then later still it was called Baneas and that is its name today. In New Testament days it was called Caesarea Philippi. It is a fascinating place, nestling at the foot of Mount Hermon which is nine thousand feet high with a snow cap all year round. At the bottom, the hill doesn't just tail out into the valley, it comes down as a cliff. From the foot of the cliff a river emerges as a sheet of water streaming out. Above this water there are niches carved into the cliff face. It has been a place where religion has been centred, a place of shrines and gods for centuries. Here there was a niche in which there was a statue of Pan – a deity supposed to have come down to earth looking something like a man.

In another niche was an image of Augustus Caesar, who was treated as god and worshipped as divine, and called "lord". There are many other niches but the statues have been taken away to museums. Here people got confused about gods who look like men and men who were supposed to be gods. It was all terribly mixed up, and the borderline between the human and the divine had become blurred and indistinct.

One day, after two-and-a-half years with his disciples, Jesus took them on a long walk and they finished up at the foot of this cliff. They must have looked at those statues of gods who look like men and men who were supposed to be gods, and Jesus asked a most important question: "Who do people say that I am?" Some wondered whether he was John the Baptist or Elijah or one of the prophets. Had he lived somewhere before? Yet Jews did not believe in reincarnation, an Eastern idea. They were groping after the truth, but they had missed it. Jesus said, "What do you think?" A fisherman looked at him and declared for the first time, "You are the Christ, the Son of the living God." Jesus was not a reincarnation of some great man; he had lived before – not on earth but in heaven.

Peter hadn't *discovered* that. The human mind is incapable of discovering the truth that Jesus is the Son of God. God had *revealed* it to Peter. Jesus had been waiting for this moment. Now he would build his church, and he changed the name of Simon (meaning "reed", something easily shaken, changeable, impetuous) to "rock" or stone (something solid you can use to build, something that would last). I am afraid that went to Peter's head and many millions since have given Peter too important a place because Jesus said these words to him. So Peter, with his big mouth still wide open, went on to rebuke Jesus for what Jesus said next, because now that it had been said, he could go and die. Now that it was known who Jesus is, he could get on with his work and go to the cross. So they would be going to Jerusalem now and Jesus was going to die and rise again.

You will never understand the cross unless you understand who Jesus is. I watched television all one Tuesday morning at the invitation of a broadcaster who said, "You poor parsons, you're always preaching when the best religious programmes are on, so we are going to put them all on one Tuesday morning. You can sit and watch them and then write and tell us what you think of them." So I did and there were two programmes on the cross. One was called "A Man Dies", a well-known dramatic presentation of the cross, and the other was called "The Davidson Affair" and presented the cross in the form of narrative reports by journalists visiting Jerusalem, interviewing Pilate in modern military uniform and so on. Both programmes were exceptionally well done, but both missed the point altogether because they never told us who Jesus is. Therefore, his death lost its meaning. You couldn't understand; you just felt sorry for the poor man who was assassinated at such an early age. You didn't realise it was the Son of God. Not knowing who he was, the viewer could not understand what he was doing on the cross. It seemed a tragedy, not a triumph. It seemed the end, not the beginning. So that is why Jesus said, "Who do you say I am?" and Peter said, "You are the Son of the living God," and Jesus said, "Peter, you are a rock. You are a stone." Here was something Jesus could build with and build on.

Thirty years later, Peter wrote this letter and now he could call Jesus what Jesus had called him. Come to him – that stone; that rock. This is one of the titles many people have given to Jesus right through the centuries.

So why did Peter call Jesus a stone, a rock, when Jesus had called him the same so many years earlier? Let us go back to the Old Testament, as Peter did, to explain what he meant. There were certain texts in the Old Testament that had a kind of picture. God is a builder and he wanted to build something on earth. I wish I could show you how they build in the Middle East, but I think I can paint it in your imagination. They use a lot of stones of all different shapes and sizes, but they begin to build by laying one stone, which is squared off and beautifully carved. They lay that at the bottom corner of the building. It holds everything else up. Then they lay another stone on top of that on the corner and then another smaller one. Then they take other stones of odd shapes and they build them against that. You sometimes see English cottages built like that, with a brick corner and then a flint infill. The stone that is vital to it all is the bottom one called the chief cornerstone and if that is not well and truly laid, then the building is going to be shaky because the stones are irregular. They all rest on and are held up by the cornerstone and the stones built on the cornerstone. You can see the picture.

In the Old Testament, God kept saying: "I'm going to lay a cornerstone in Israel; I'm going to lay something you can build on." Peter says that God was talking about Jesus. Jesus is that cornerstone. For no other foundation can anyone lay than that which is laid – Jesus. So Peter is now saying: Build on Jesus. This implies: Jesus said he could build on me but I am building on Jesus; I am just another stone on top and you are all living stones, all built on the same thing. There is a picture building up here of a new building, but the cornerstone is the key. A new church building in Guildford had the entire roof resting on one corner pillar of reinforced concrete. Three-and-a-half tons of steel went into a pillar to hold the whole thing up. When I looked at that I thought of Jesus – the whole resting on that solid corner, holding us all up, protecting us all.

Now this is the picture that Peter wants you to get hold of. We are looking at Jesus as a rock, someone you can build your life on, as somebody who is utterly solid and reliable. As a stone chosen by God – very precious, carefully laid.

If I may put it reverently, he was laid in the womb of the Virgin Mary, and God was laying in Zion a cornerstone for people to build on.

Peter is saying that you can do two things with Jesus: you can build on him or you can say, "I can build without him." You can either say, "I'm going to build my life on Jesus, he is going to be the heart of it, it will all rest on Jesus – everything I add to my life will rest on him" or you might say "I can build my own life, I can do without a cornerstone, I can manage my own affairs." The tragedy is that men and women are doing just this – "... the stone which the builders rejected." The politicians are not using Jesus to build a stable society for us and our children. The scientists don't use Jesus to build a new world in which discoveries that they make are used for good and for the benefit of mankind. There are many teachers trying to educate children who are not building on Jesus. So we are desperately trying to build a world that is safe and clean and pure and peaceful without Jesus. In the UN building in New York there is an empty room. They decided when they put up that building that they would put a room for worship at the heart of it. The biggest debate the United Nations ever had was what to put in there. Some said they wanted a cross but that wasn't acceptable to others. Others wanted some flowers but that is not acceptable to Muslims. They finished with just a block of stone and it means nothing. How one wishes it meant the Rock of Ages. The United Nations will never succeed unless they build on Jesus.

The world cannot succeed unless it is built on Jesus, and neither can your life or mine. Here is the point Peter is making: if you decide to try to build without Jesus and leave this stone on one side, you will trip over it. The stone which the builders rejected, which God has made the head cornerstone, is the stone which to others becomes a rock of stumbling. It is almost a humorous picture. It's as if a bricklayer looks at a brick and says, "Well, no I don't like that brick very much," and puts it down. The next time he walks around the building, he falls over the brick. If I do not build my life up on Jesus then one day Jesus will pull it down. I will stumble and fall. There is going to come an almighty crash to any life that is not built on the cornerstone of Jesus, and he will cause the crash. The reason is this: he came once to be our Saviour to build us up and he will come a second time to judge and to pull men down. The same stone that could be used as a foundation for them will become a rock of offence and they will trip over and fall because of Jesus. This means that you cannot ignore Jesus. You either build on him or he brings you down. You either accept him now as your Saviour and find that your life has a foundation and a stability that you can build on, or one day he will say to you: "Depart from me, I do not know you. Your life is finished; your life is over. I do not know you." It is an awe-inspiring thought that those who believe are not put to shame. You will never be disappointed in Jesus, but those who reject him will find that one day, over they go.

The other side is this: when you believe in him, you become a living stone; you become rock; you become stable; you become built into something else. Peter now begins to mix his metaphors so much. He gives picture after picture of what happens when people believe in Jesus. First: they are built into a spiritual house; and there is the cornerstone; but then more and more believers are built in. You become a house. A house for whom? A house is only built for someone to live in and it is a house of God, made up of living stones (not a physical structure). Jesus is a living stone; we are living stones. You will never see a monument engraved, "In memory of Jesus Christ." You can see the monuments to Jesus around you when you worship together with other believers. He lives in his people; we are a spiritual house. The Spartan king was once showing an enemy round his city and the enemy saw the soldiers. The king said, "You see these men? They are the walls of Sparta" – in other words, we don't have stone walls, we have human walls. Where does God live on earth? His people are his walls and he lives in them and among them.

Let us now look at the second picture. You are not only a spiritual house; you have become a *holy priesthood*. In Old Testament days they had priests. If you wanted to get through to God you had to find a priest who would take an animal and sacrifice it for you. Those days are gone since you became living stones. Every living stone becomes a holy priest. All God's children are priests now. As soon as you start building on Jesus the cornerstone, you become a holy priesthood. I don't need a priest to hear me confess my sins. I don't need a priest to get through to God for me. I can get straight through. What a freedom to come right into the presence of God into the holy of holies, to bring my little offering right to him. Every living stone is part of a holy priesthood.

Then look at the next picture: you are a chosen race. Think of that. There are only two nations on the earth: believers and unbelievers. Once you are building on Christ the chief cornerstone, you have become a holy nation, the chosen race. God chose us. I am amazed – why did God choose me? Why did he choose you? I don't know. It is a rock of stumbling to people who don't believe in Jesus, but those who build on Jesus the cornerstone say, "Marvellous! God chose little me to fit in just here. He chose, and so I am a very precious stone in God's sight."

You are a spiritual house, you are a holy priesthood, and you are a chosen race. Why? Peter says to do two things: offer spiritual sacrifices to God and declare to other people the wonderful things that God can do for them. Those are two things the world cannot understand the church doing. These are the two very things that the world would rather we didn't do. Take the first: to *offer spiritual sacrifices*. We are not holding services to give members a good time but to give God a good time. We do not set out to entertain men but to glorify God. When we are singing our hymns we are offering spiritual sacrifices to God as his priests. The world says you would do far more good if you went out and helped someone. They don't believe in God, they don't think God has feelings. They don't realise that God loves to listen to us. You are being built into Jesus so that you might offer spiritual sacrifices God wants to receive from you.

We are to tell people three things. First, when Jesus is the foundation of your life, you step out of darkness into light. Second, you who were a nobody have become somebody. Third, you who had only received justice now receive mercy. We are told to go out and tell the world those three wonderful things. Darkness into light first. Do you know that before you became a Christian, you walked in mental darkness? You could not understand or see things. If somebody talked to you about the Bible, you would have said, "I just don't see it. I can't see what you're getting at." But as a believer you have stepped out of mental darkness into mental light.

There was another sort of darkness you walked into—moral darkness. By this I mean you did not realise how bad you were. You couldn't see that either. You were groping around in the shadows, doing things that are best done in the dark, things that you wouldn't have liked everybody else to know, thinking thoughts that you wouldn't have liked everybody to see. I remember a most challenging thing once being said by a preacher I was listening to. He said, "Which of you would like all the thoughts of the last week that you have had made into a film and shown to the congregation?

Which of you would like all the words you have said taken down on a tape recorder and played through to everybody?" We once were in darkness, but the marvellous love of God lifted us out of the darkness, switched the light on, and we saw mentally and morally – we realised where we were and the light showed us the way out.

Tell them too that once you were no people and now you are some people, his people. Isn't it marvellous to belong? Until you know Jesus you are an orphan. You may marry another orphan and be very happy for a few years but only until "death us do part". You may have a lot of friends who are also orphans and you can hold each other up for a time, but deep down you know that you are all alone, you are going out into the unknown alone, and you will make the last journey of life alone.

You who were nobody – no people – did not belong. It is a phrase from the prophet Hosea. Have you ever read that amazing book? It is quite a story. If it were published today in the Sunday papers it would be under the headline, "Preacher Marries Prostitute". For that is what happened. Hosea was told by God to go and marry a woman of the streets and he did. There were three children born. The first one was his, and the second one was not his. Hosea called that second child "not my people". God's message was: "Hosea, I want you to get up and preach, and I want you to tell the people of Israel they are not my people, I am not their father, and tell them to come back and be my people. They will listen to you because they have seen this lived out in your own household and they will understand." Hosea said this publicly: "This little child's not mine, and you're not God's. Come back to him; come to him."

We are to tell the world: you are no people, you don't belong to God, but come to him; come to Jesus that living stone, and you will be God's people, a chosen race, special people whom he values and cherishes.

The third thing we are to tell people is that outside of Christ the only thing you can expect from God is justice, and in Christ you can receive mercy. Justice is to get what I deserve; mercy is to get what I don't deserve. People ask me questions that imply that God is unjust. I tell you that God is absolutely just – but who wants justice? Which of us is prepared to stand before God and say, "God, all I ask is justice, and I know I will get to heaven." If it is justice that he is giving us, then it is hell for all of us. But when you come to him, that living stone, you start building your life on him. What do you find? You receive mercy.

I won't tell you the circumstances, but I remember seeing a woman down on the ground crying out, "Mercy, mercy, mercy," and the word really meant something. She had done something and she deserved serious punishment, but she was pleading and she meant it. You can have mercy from God. Christ took the cross so that you can receive mercy. God can be merciful to a sinner, and he is, as soon as that person asks for mercy.

As soon as you come to Christ, that living stone, you get built in with other living stones into this holy priesthood, this chosen race, this spiritual house that is going to be a group of people who offer spiritual sacrifices to God and tell the world about light, and about mercy, and about belonging to God the Father.

1 Peter 2:11–17

This little passage brings us down to earth with a bump. We have been looking at what God thinks about Christians. Now we are going to look at what people think about Christians. It is not only important what God sees in us, but it is important what others think about us, and our *behaviour* is going to decide that one.

I want to affirm two things now. Firstly, the fact that I belong to a heavenly country must affect my private behaviour; and the fact that I belong to an earthly country must change my public behaviour. A Christian's behaviour is in these two departments, private and public. It is because I am a citizen of glory and heaven that I must watch my private behaviour; it is because I am a citizen of earth that I must watch my public behaviour. Peter, writing to these Christians, speaks first about their private behaviour and he calls them exiles and aliens. The word "alien" means someone who has come from another country, and the word "exile" means someone who is hoping to go back to their country. I am both and so are you, if you are a believer. We are aliens because our life is from heaven. We have been born again of God, and our life belongs up there. We don't belong here; we are misfits. You discover that very quickly after you become a Christian. In your first few weeks and months as a Christian you think everybody is going to be as thrilled and happy as you are that you have been converted. Then you begin to find your friends dropping off. You begin to find you are not as popular as you were, and you realise you are different and they feel it. You are an alien; you belong to another country. You also realise that you are an exile because that country more and more becomes the place that you are longing to go to. Which of us Christians wouldn't be off to heaven tomorrow if we got the chance? Wouldn't it be wonderful if God told you "You're coming to heaven tomorrow?" We could hardly wait to tell everybody and say, "You must come with us." We are exiles. We don't belong here. Our life comes from heaven, and we want to get back there with it as soon as we can.

The Jews knew the meaning of those two words—for two

thousand years they have been aliens and exiles wherever they have been. It is a fact that when you are different from others around you, you are much more likely to come under criticism; you are much more likely to have rumours started about yourself. The Jews have been through all this, but Christians know it too. Charles Wesley writes in one of his hymns, "Strangers and pilgrims here below, this earth we know is not our place." We don't belong anymore. A Christian is a social misfit.

One of the dangers of living in a country that is not your own is "going native". Sometimes British troops were so long overseas that they "went native" and when they came back to England they couldn't adjust to English life again. They were adjusted to the country of their exile too much, and therefore their own country had ceased to be really home – and that can happen to Christians. We have got to spend the rest of the days of this life in this earth where we don't belong. The danger is that we will "go native" and settle down.

So Peter is saying: I beg you, I beseech you, I appeal to you as aliens and exiles.... And this implies two things: negatively to abstain from certain things; positively to maintain certain things. You are to abstain from certain things which everybody else around you will be doing, and to abstain from those appetites which everybody else satisfies around you, which you must not. For there are certain appetites which, if they get out of hand, destroy your spiritual life; they are enemies of your soul. It is vital that you should not "go native". It is vital that, even though everybody else around you is indulging these appetites, you don't, that you keep this spiritual warfare on your side and that you don't lose the battle. The Christian knows that life on earth is going to be a battle, not a picnic. It is going to be a tough fight, and the biggest fight you will have is with yourself. You will have battles with other people, but there are those appetites within yourself that are appealed to by the world in which you live, and it is very difficult to resist. Peter is telling believers to abstain from those passions which are going to kill your soul. There are certain things a Christian can no longer do; if he does, he will "go native". He will cease to be an exile, and he will be sorry to leave earth one day because he will have got bound to it. That is the negative side: the appetites.

The positive side concerns our actions. A Christian must not just be a negative person who says, "Oh no, I don't do this, and I don't do that. No thank you, I don't touch that." That is something that will never commend itself by itself to the world around. So Peter adds the balance and he also tells Christians to maintain good conduct. The word "good" here needs looking at. There are two words for "good" in the Greek language and one means something that is upright, clean, straight – but that is not the word used here. The word used here means "attractive; winsome", the kind of goodness that even the world will like. It means the kind of morality of which the world will say, "Now that is how I would like to be." You can have a negative abstaining from wrong things that puts the world off – a person who has a long list of what they never do and never touch. But unless that is balanced with maintaining attractive, winsome goodness, then the world is not going to come to Christ.

You see the balance here – what delightful teaching this is. You may say, "I have kept away from all the things that are wrong," but unless you can say, "But my goodness is attractive," then two things will happen. First of all, you will be criticised and secondly, so will God. Therefore, we are told to maintain good conduct, to silence the criticism, and to help people to praise. This will shut their mouths if they are going to talk about you in a wrong way and open their mouths if they are going to talk about God.

The aspect of public behaviour comes from the fact that I belong to an earthly country. A man was arrested in the US for a particularly horrible crime, and he claimed diplomatic immunity. He said, "I am the son of a foreign diplomat and therefore I claim diplomatic immunity." It did not exactly help the reputation of his country that he said, "I belong to another country; therefore, I can do what I like in this one." You can't do that.

A Christian, even though he belongs to heaven, must never say, "I can do what I like on earth because I'm not a citizen here. I belong to God, I have nothing to do with politics, I have nothing to do with the state, I have nothing to do with the community because I belong to heaven." That is not Christian talk. The Christian belongs to an earthly country as well as a heavenly one. He is a citizen of two states: the kingdom of God and the state in which he is a citizen. I have two "passports" and I need both. I am a citizen of two countries. I have a certificate of my baptism and I also have a national insurance card. I belong to two countries at the moment and I have a duty to both. No Christian can make his heavenly citizenship an excuse for doing wrong down here.

Here we have some remarkable teaching. First of all, we are told about the matter of allegiance—that every Christian has a duty to submit to the government that is running his country. Many of us know situations where it is difficult to do this, and when there is a conflict, we must obey God. It is God's will that there be a government and that there be ministers of state. Alas on my passport there appears the title "Minister of Religion" which gets me into difficulties crossing certain borders. But there are two people who are entitled to call themselves "ministers" – ministers of religion and ministers of state. The Bible applies the word "minister" to the government; those set in authority over us are ministers of God and their job is not to give us more money in our pockets, not to give us a healthier economy, but to restrain evil and to promote good. That is the government's job, and it is there in scripture, in 1 Peter. Her Majesty's government will one day stand before God. He will say, "You were the government in England. I allowed you to be chosen. Did you do your job? Did you restrain evil and promote good?" That is the job of Her Majesty's government, and because that is the job of the government, a Christian is to pray for that government, to pay taxes to that government and, what is desperately needed today, to give respect to those who are in authority over us. This is Bible teaching.

Therefore, a Christian has this duty of giving his allegiance to the powers that be. The interesting thing is that Peter wrote this when Nero was the emperor, and it was as a result of Nero's persecution that Peter was to die in Rome. Yet he said: "Give respect and allegiance." It is for this reason that the early Christians could say when they were hauled before the courts to the emperor, "Christians are your best citizens." Does that mean that a Christian must never disobey the authority? No, there comes a line, and I will tell you what it is. When a government tells you not to do something that God has told you to do, a Christian has no choice. A Christian must then say, as Peter said in his own lifetime, "We must obey God rather than men." God has said, "Go and preach my gospel to every creature." God has said, "Go and spread my Word everywhere," and if a government says you must not preach about Jesus and you must not spread his Word, then a Christian has to say, "We must obey God rather than men." For the government that says that no longer has God's authority behind it. Those who are troubled about the smuggling of Bibles into other countries need to remember that we would not have the Bible in England unless it had one day been smuggled in here, in cotton bales through King's Lynn, Norfolk, in the days when you would be burned alive if you were caught reading this book. There were those, thank God, who smuggled the Bible into England in English, and we got the gospel.

Because there comes a point where a government oversteps its responsibility. Our government does not forbid the sale of Bibles. Shame on us that we don't use our freedom more but there are governments that do. What should a Christian do then? A Christian says, like Shadrach, Meshach and Abednego, "Our God is able to deliver us, but even if he doesn't, we will go on. We will worship and serve him." But until we cross that line, a Christian is to give allegiance to the government. We believe that God overrules and that he has in his hands the affairs of the nations.

Why do we do this? Again, because of uninformed criticism — that there may be no accusation of political subversion. Pray very hard for Christians in many countries who are faced daily with this impossible question: "Do I obey this or do I not?" Christians have divided over the answer and we must pray for them in the agony of deciding when it is a compromise and when it is right to obey the government.

Finally, our attitude is to be one of *respect*. I think you can sum up the Ten Commandments in that one word. Respect God — respect his name; respect him. Respect your neighbour — his life, his wife, his property, his reputation. This is one of those things that is in very short supply today. If there is one proof that our nation is a long, long way from God, it is the lack of respect – respect for older people on the part of younger people, respect for younger people on the part of older people, respect for those in authority and political office on the part of the electorate, respect for the electorate on the part of those in authority.

Indeed, the mass media seems to have got into the hands of those whose open aim is to destroy respect. But here we have it: *honour* all men. It does not matter whether someone is rich or poor, educated or simple, honour him. He or she is made in the image of God. Honor all men; love the brotherhood. Coming in from the wide circle of mankind, there is an even deeper respect that Christians have for one another: love the brotherhood.

Every Christian, wherever they are, must balance two responsibilities: they can neither be so earthly that they are no heavenly use, nor so heavenly-minded that they are no earthly use. They must live in both countries – aliens and exiles with a loyalty to God and to the government and to see that respect is spread abroad in our land.

5

SUBMISSION

Read 1 Peter 2:18–3:7

A. SLAVES TO MASTERS

    1. Submission (18)
        a. Kind/gentle. Good master tough
        b. Overbearing. Bad master tender
    2. Suffering (19–20)
        a. Receive God's approval
            i. Mindful of God; ii. Take it patiently
        b. Follow Christ's example
            i. His innocence; ii. His silence
    3. Substitution (21–25)
        a. Saviour dying – done with sin
            i. Die to sin; ii. live to righteousness
        b. Shepherd living – done with self
            i. Not straying; ii. But following

B. WIVES TO HUSBANDS

    1. Wives (1–6)
        a. What?
            i. Attitude
                Submissive; reverent; chaste
            ii. Adornment
                Not outward (hair, jewellery, clothes)
                But inward (gentle, quiet)
        b. Why?
            i. Unbelieving husbands; ii. Believing husbands
    2. Husbands (7)
        a. What?
            i. Consideration ii. Courtesy
        b. Why?
            i. Inheritance; ii. Intercession

The first part of this passage is concerned basically with a Christian's attitude to work. I suppose that most of us spend about a third of our life in bed, another third of our life at work and the rest of our time is nearly our own to eat and to play, to be with our family and to do all the odd jobs around the house, to worship, to go to church, to be at meetings. Wouldn't it be a tragedy if we saw Christianity as limited to that third of our life, which we call leisure? That would mean two-thirds of our life that God gave us is beyond the reach of Christ, beyond being used for him. I could teach on how to use the hours of sleep for Jesus. There is a marvellous text in the book of Psalms which says, "He gives to his beloved in sleep." You can use your sleep for the Lord, but we are concerned now with using the hours that you spend at work. I am concerned that you should have those used for Christ. Otherwise, all that part of your life is wasted, just filling in time, getting a bit of money so that you can then be a Christian in your leisure time. But when 1 Peter was written, people didn't have any leisure. They were on a seven-day week. The Romans, it is true, had a holiday once a month, but that was only for the citizens.

Most of the Christians in the early church were slaves and they had a seven-day working week. It may come as a surprise to you that for the first three hundred years of Christianity, Sunday was not a day of rest. They felt no contradiction in that, it just meant that they had to hold Sunday services at four in the morning and ten at night. That is what they did for the first three centuries, but my, how the church grew during that time!

They had to find their Christian vocation in their work. Nor could they choose their job. There is an idea around today that vocational calling means that Christ chooses what job you do. It is very difficult to find any justification for that view in the Bible – that Christ tells you to be this, that or the other. What the Bible does say is that your Christian vocation, whatever your job, is to do your job *for Jesus* – that is what "calling" means.

A new Christian might be saying to me, "Well, at the moment I work in a factory or a shop and I'm seeking the Lord's will as to what job I should do." I would then say: I can tell you what the Lord's will is for you: that you do the job you are doing for him, whatever that job might be – that is a Christian vocation.

There are five things about our work in this passage that I am going to underline. The first thing about the Christian life is that it is a life of *service*. That word "servant" is not very popular. Who wants to be a servant today? But this was written to those who are called to serve and the first word of v. 18 is, literally, "slaves". A slave had no time off, no money, no leisure and no marriage rights. A slave belonged to his master twenty-four hours a day. The master could claim any time in that day for hard work. Most of the early Christians were slaves. In the Roman Empire there were sixty million slaves. Two out of every three people you met in the streets were slaves and they had no rights whatsoever. Can you imagine the popularity of New Testament teaching when people like Peter came along and said, "Slaves, be submissive"? That is not likely to be popular teaching.

There were people in those days who led the civil rights movement, the "freedom fighters". They led one slave revolt, which the Romans crushed, and as they did so they killed forty thousand slaves. The early Christians were not "freedom fighters". They did not march for civil rights.

Those early Christians said, "If you're a slave, submit." They said it firstly because Christ called himself a servant. They considered it was dignified to be a servant of others. Jesus said, "I didn't come to be ministered unto, I came to minister." He referred to himself many Old Testament scriptures from the prophet Isaiah, which described the Son of God as "God's servant". The dignity of service is something that Jesus introduced into a world that denied it. Everybody's ambition was to own a slave so that they could be free for leisure. Every Greek and Roman wanted to be able to be free and have all the leisure in the world and washing up done for them by slaves. The price for a slave was thirty pieces of silver. Judas, when he sold our Lord for thirty pieces, was asking for the price of a slave so that he could have a slave and then he could be free for leisure. It is very interesting to see how his mind was working.

So you get the ambition in the ancient Greek and Roman world not to work and to have loads of time on their hands to do what they wanted to do. There is the same kind of ambition today: pleading for less work and more leisure. Whatever are people going to find to do in all the rest of their time? Boredom is a problem and has to be filled up with entertainment. It is almost uncomfortable to read the commandment: "Remember the Sabbath day to keep it holy." In other words, give one day in seven to God, because it begins: "six days shalt thou labour". When you read it today that is more uncomfortable than the clause about giving the seventh to God.

God is at work – let us start there. God is a worker. But God rested from his work in making man in his image. It is a divine principle that people need a rest, and God has told us that a weekly rest is the ideal for us. Jesus Christ, the Son of God, came as a worker and said, "My father works until now and now I work", and we are called as followers of Jesus to work, to serve, and to be servants of others. There is nothing menial in that, there is a holy dignity. Ever since Christ took a towel and washed people's dirty feet, there is a dignity in service and in working with your hands. Jesus worked with his hands for eighteen years, Paul worked with his hands. Where did we get the idea that somebody who wears a collar and tie and pushes a pen is somehow better than a man who uses his hands for work? We didn't get that from Jesus, and we didn't get it from the New Testament where Paul boasts that he worked with his hands to provide for his own needs and the needs of others. Therefore, we are called to a life of service. There can be no greater calling in the human community than to serve other people in their needs – not to serve yourself, but to serve others in the name of the Lord.

The second thing that we are told is that it is a life of *submission*. That, too, seems like a humiliating word. People say, "I want to be free; I want to be my own boss. I'd love to work for myself and not for that old man who sits in the next office. I would love to be independent." But we are called to live a life of submission – of giving in, allowing someone else to control you. That again is far from popular today, it wasn't popular then either.

Bosses are on a spectrum, from those who are kind, gentle, considerate, fair and reasonable to those who are just the opposite, who are despotic, cruel, unfair, harsh, and autocratic. Christians are called to be submissive to both. Now which is harder? I think the temptation, if you have got a nice, considerate reasonable boss, is to be overly familiar, to take advantage of the relationship, to be too pally, but there are dangers with the other sort too. There are dangers in becoming sulky and resentful, doing your work in a half-hearted way, doing it slowly, doing it badly and reluctantly, only interested in the wage packet and the clock ticking round until the time you can go. Peter is saying that you are called to a life of service and submission. If you have a boss, it does not matter to God what kind of a boss it is, you are employed by him and you do your work as unto the Lord – gladly, eagerly, willingly. You may have the privilege of being your own boss but many have very difficult people over them and go into the place of work on Monday morning wondering what mood the boss is in. It doesn't matter what mood he or she is in. Peter is saying that as a Christian there is one mood for you to be in, and only one. That is to do a good job for your boss, Jesus.

There was a factory in Latin America where a large number of people in the factory were converted. They became known as the "hallelujah boys". The employer, the boss of the factory was approached and asked what he thought about these Christians in his factory. He didn't understand the question at first and then he said, "Oh, you mean the hallelujah boys? They're the best workers we've got. In fact, Jesus is the best foreman in this factory." What a tribute!

I remember a young man who used to play the organ at the church in which I was pastor. He had been taken out of a good job as an accountant and had been put in Her Majesty's forces. He had been conscripted and he was put in the pay office scribbling out wage slips for soldiers. I remember one day talking to the officer in charge of the accounts department. We were chatting away and he was asking me what good the church did – the usual kind of question. I said, "Look, do you know so and so in your office?" He said, "Yes." I said, "What do you think of him?" He said, "He's the best worker we've got." And I said, "Well, that's what the church is doing."

This ought to be the mark; this ought to distinguish Christians. Are you worried as to how you should let people know you're a Christian at work? Here is a very easy way: just do your work for the Lord and they will notice a difference straight away. They will see something quite unusual: submission. A life of submission is not easy. Don't get me wrong, it will not pay; there will be times when you submit to a difficult employer, he will take advantage of it and you will suffer unjustly.

We come to the third mark of a Christian at work. It is also going to be a life of *suffering*. Of course you will suffer, and undeserved suffering will come your way. Peter says that there is no credit if you do something wrong and then the boss tears a strip off you for that. But supposing he is in a bad mood and tells you off for doing something that you didn't do. Or because he is in a bad temper he criticises some work that you have done well and to the best of your ability and you know is right; he humbles you in front of the other workers, ridicules you because you are a Christian. God notices that. A man ought to be patient if he is suffering because he deserves it. But if you can suffer in an undeserved way, suffer the injustice of life at work and still remain patient, then you don't need to worry that you have been unjustly treated by men – God saw it. What more do you need? That relieves the pain and anxiety. Apart from anything else, you are learning to walk in the steps of Jesus.

If you have a good boss, then you don't have such an opportunity to follow Jesus as somebody with a bad boss. If you never suffer unjustly at work, then you don't have the opportunity that Peter describes here of winning God's approval because you are following Christ's example. What is his example? They spat on him, they reviled him, they knocked him down, they stripped him, they whipped him. Look what they did to him, and what did he do to them? He just said, "Father, forgive them, they know not what they do." When he was reviled, he reviled not again. You are called to a life of unjust suffering. I would say that if you follow Christ as you ought to, sooner or later you will suffer in an undeserved way in the Christian life – either at work or somewhere else, maybe at home. Don't worry about that, Christ did and you are following in his footsteps.

Fourthly, you are called to a life of *substitution*. When Christ suffered unjustly, what was he doing? The answer is that he was exchanging his life for ours, and we are called to exchange ours for his. When Jesus suffered even though he didn't deserve it, our sins were being put on him. The other side of that is that as he took our sins, we are to take his life of righteousness and goodness. Every day of my life, I am to exchange my life for his. He took my sin on him and suffered unjustly. Therefore, I take his goodness upon me and suffer unjustly. Have you got the exchange? This is what is known as the substituted life: I live, yet no longer I but Christ lives within me. We have literally changed places. On the cross he took my place; at the office tomorrow morning, I take his. Do you see the secret of living the Christian life? It is a life of service, it is a life of submission; he served, he submitted. It is a life of suffering: he suffered, we suffer. It is a life of substitution: he took my life of sin so that I might take his life of righteousness. He bore my sins in his body on the tree that I might bear his life in my body at the office. That is what Peter is teaching.

Finally, here is the fifth thing and it is so simple: you will never manage this on your own. The fifth part of the life of a Christian at work is that he needs a shepherd. When you are on your own you wander around like lost sheep; you stray around into all kinds of situations and circumstances; you need a shepherd. You need someone to stand right by you the whole day. It may be a very good thing as you go into the office or shop tomorrow morning to say, "The Lord is my Shepherd, I shall not want. He's going to lead me today.

He's going to make me be busy, he's going to make me lie down at tea break and have a rest. He's going to go right with me through a valley of darkness today. When I'm attacked, he's going to protect me. He's going to keep refreshing me and anointing me with his Holy Spirit. He's going to lead me right through today and at the end of the day, we're going home together." You need a shepherd!

These then are the five marks of a Christian at work. He works because he has been called to service. Every Christian is a servant, called to serve others. He is submissive to those in authority over him, whether they be good or bad; whether they be kind or cruel. Whether they are easy to get on with or most difficult, we are called to suffer. There will be times, maybe before next Sunday, when life is dreadfully unfair to you, when you feel resentful and bitter and frustrated because you were overlooked for that higher post or because someone else spoiled your work. You might feel bitter but remember that God saw it and he approves because you are following in Christ's footsteps. You are called to a life of substitution so that though your body walks into the office, it is Christ who walks through that door. Having taken your sinful life on himself, he says, "Now you take my life into you." Finally, having exchanged lives he says: "I'll come with you and I'll be your Shepherd. I'll be the guardian of your soul and I'll keep you spiritually while you're going through all that at work tomorrow."

Now we turn from our duty at work to our duty at home. Here are six verses for the wives and one for the husbands, but frankly if we husbands lived up to the one verse for us, then our wives would be very happy to live up to theirs. Some years ago, a child psychologist, after studying a number of children with serious problems, came to the conclusion that it is more important for parents to love each other than for parents to love their children. The relationship between husband and wife will have a far deeper effect on the child's feeling of security or insecurity than anything either parent does for the children. I have lived long enough and talked to enough people with problems to know that this is true. The fundamental foundation for a home is the relationship between the husband and wife. If that relationship is right, then the other things will tend to follow.

We are zooming in ever more closely to the personal nature of working out the Christian life. The first thing we notice is that a happy home is not based on things, possessions, but on people. One of the greatest tragedies of our affluent society is that we have so often thought that an ideal home was made up of possessions, furnishings and kitchen equipment. Then perhaps we wake up too late and find that our young people have gone astray and they are in trouble. We realise we were so busy putting the house right that we never built a home where they felt at home. We created the kind of place they didn't want to be in and they wanted to get away from.

Bear in mind that we know for certain Peter was married because he had a mother-in-law. She is mentioned in the Gospels and she was one of the first to feel the healing touch of Jesus upon her. She lay sick of a fever and he went into the home and put her on her feet again.

That was one of the first experiences Peter had of Jesus' power. As a married man, Peter knew what he was talking about. Yet the extraordinary thing is that Peter says exactly the same things as Paul says and as John says. You find indeed that Christians say the same thing about marriage: there is a God-given pattern for a marriage relationship and it is the ideal home pattern.

First of all the wives. Do you notice that in both cases, Peter talks about responsibilities and not rights? One of the things that wrecks a marriage relationship is to talk about "my rights". I have a right to this or that. But the Bible does not talk that way. The Bible says, "Wife, you have responsibilities. Husband, you have responsibilities." It is a list of responsibilities that we have here. Wives, what should you be? We are now going to get not very popular advice but some very good advice. It concerns two things in the wife: her *attitude* and her *adornment* – her attitude to her husband and her adornment to herself.

Three adjectives are used here: *submissive*, *reverent*, *chaste*. If I give you the adjectives that are opposite to these words, you will understand the kind of wife you are not to be. Peter is really saying you are not to be an aggressive, contemptuous, flirtatious wife. The three words he uses are the opposite of those and as soon as I have used those three negative words, you think "Dear me, what a wife!" Rightly so, for that is the very picture of what a wife ought not to be.

The word, "submissive" causes difficulty straightaway. In the days when everybody is talking about equality and the word "obey" has been officially cut out of many wedding services, it is considered terribly old-fashioned to use this word "submissive". It seems to us a cringing word, a crawling word, and we don't like it. Yet here in God's Word is what I would call a voluntary selflessness, which is enjoined on wives who are Christians. It means that in accepting marriage you were accepting leadership. You were expecting a man to whom you would look to make decisions. If I speak to girls who are not yet married and are looking for a husband, I say: don't marry someone you can't look up to. If he is not superior to you morally and spiritually, someone you feel could lead you, then don't marry him. Indeed, that is the most important thing.

It is not just enough that you be Christians together. Is he a person to whom you can look up? A person whose leadership you could accept, a person whose guidance you would find helpful? That is the point of being engaged first, to find out if he is that kind of a person. There is going to be something wrong and even ungodly in a relationship in which you have to take the lead. That is not God's pattern and it is wrong. We used to talk about her wearing the trousers, but that phrase has somehow gone out a bit, but the meaning is still there and it is used as a criticism and rightly so.

The second adjective, "reverent", is not primarily a religious word. You are going to see your husband at his worst. You're going to find out all his faults and weaknesses. You are going to know him better than anyone else. This is really saying: "See that throughout your relationship, you go on looking up to him, respecting him." That requires great grace when you find out all about your husband and live with him long enough to know what he is really like. See that you are submissive, reverent, and chaste. The words used in the marriage service are, "And keep you only unto him so long as you both shall live."

Why should you be like this? First of all, Peter says your husband may not be a Christian. If he is not a Christian, this is the way to win him: not to preach at him, you are to win him without a word. How many wives have learned the hard way that you will never win your husband to Christ by preaching at him? You have to win him without a word, and you will do it by having this kind of attitude towards him even though he is not a Christian. It is not the right thing for a Christian wife to say, "I can't respect my husband, he's not a Christian. I can't submit to my husband, he's not a Christian." The Bible teaches: be submissive and you might win him for Christ. That is the approach.

How do girls ever get to be married to those who are not Christians? There are three ways in which it happens; one of which is a good way, and the other two are not. Some girls are married to those who are not Christians because they have been converted since they married and that is perfectly alright. They married, and then later they came to Christ and this happens frequently because the most difficult person to lead to Christ is a man in his middle age. In our middle age we men are proud, self-sufficient creatures. We are not when we are young, we are not when we are old, but in the middle years to admit that we need help is the hardest thing to do. Therefore, it is more likely that wives will be converted first in the middle years, and many are.

So that is one way that young women get into a marriage with someone who is not a Christian. The second way that they can get into such a relationship is by being deceived by the boy, and that happens very frequently because the boy will come to church with the girl during their courtship. Why? Because the girl is in church and he wants to be with her, and that is why he comes. Wives have said to me, "I don't understand it. My husband came with me to church and seemed to enjoy it right until the marriage. Then as soon as we got back from the honeymoon he said, 'Now you go, and I'll stay home and look after the dog,' and later he looked after the children." Many think that because a boy comes to church with her while they are courting, he is a Christian.

The third way in which a girl can get into this is by simple disobedience and going against the Word and the will of God and deliberately, knowingly, marrying someone who is not a Christian. However a girl has got into this situation, it must be her deepest desire and longing to bring her husband to Christ. If she doesn't then it is going to be an increasing strain to live together; to come home from a service when you have been bursting with love for God and you long to share it and talk over what God has said and done for you, and not be able to must be dreadful. To want to share things together, to pray together about a problem and have someone who is too proud to get on his knees with you is very difficult.

So of course, every Christian wife longs to win her husband for Christ. How is she going to do it? She must do it without a word, just by being the best possible kind of wife to him.

The second thing that will come up here is *adornment*. Now Peter makes it quite clear that every wife should be concerned about her beauty. Peter says this. He doesn't say it doesn't matter whether you are beautiful or not, he says you should be concerned with beauty. But what kind of beauty concerns should you have? Now here he is talking as a married man, and he's not just talking about money. He says that it should not depend on clothes or jewellery or hairdos. He doesn't say you are not to have them, but it should not depend on that. What kind of beauty should a wife seek? The beauty not of outward adornment – because that is all put on, and what is put on comes off, and the husband is going to see the wife when it comes off and not just when it is on. It is put on when they go out and it comes off when they come home. What is the beauty that Peter is concerned about? It is the beauty that comes from within and comes out. That is a different kind of beauty. The other you lose; this you gain.

It was Dr. W.E. Sangster who shocked his church by announcing he was going to hold a beauty queen contest in the church, but that there was to be one limitation on entrance: that everyone had to be over sixty years of age. He was seeking to demonstrate the difference between glamour and beauty—the beauty of a meek and gentle spirit. In other words, the beauty that comes out later like the beauty of a butterfly wrapped in the chrysalis that forms within, and blossoms out. That is the kind of beauty that every wife should be anxious to possess. For in this way, her husband will become more and more proud of her as the years pass. You can have the beauty that comes more and more out in character. This beauty of a precious jewel, which in God's sight is very precious—that is the kind of jewellery to possess and it doesn't cost you any money. It does cost you some time, and it does cost you effort, but that is the beauty that Peter advises. Why? Because, he said, this is the secret of the godly women of old.

Sarah was one such. Do you know what Sarah's nickname for Abraham was? "Lord". What a nickname to give your husband! I am not suggesting wives should call their husbands "Lord so and so", but, you see, the nickname showed what she thought of him. Her attitude, a meek and gentle spirit, came out in that nickname. This was the secret of the holy women of old. If you read the early chapters of Genesis, you find that the patriarchs had wives who were fair to look upon. Then what comes as a bit of a shock to you is to discover that when that is said, they are eighty years of age. This is the secret and this is the beauty, which will go on enabling your husband to be proud of you.

That is enough for the wives. One of the revolutionary things in the Bible that you will not find in any other book in the ancient world is this: husbands and wives have duties to each other. That is a revolution in thinking about marriage in the ancient world. It was Christ who made it possible. Before that, wives were considered to have duties to husbands, but husbands were not considered to have duties to wives. Indeed, this is the revolutionary teaching that comes into life through the Bible and transforms marriage. In other words, in the realm of duty, husbands and wives are equal – they have a duty to each other and that makes a world of difference. The wife is not a drudge, or a housekeeper, or a child bearer, or a plaything. She is a person to whom the husband has responsibilities as she has towards him.

What are they? The first thing is *consideration*. That word means "a very practical knowledge", a knowledge that not all of us husbands have. It doesn't come naturally or automatically; it is a knowledge that is learned. Here I want to be utterly practical. The word translated "live" is elsewhere translated "having physical relations." To "dwell together" in the Bible primarily refers to physical relations. To live together considerately means that the husband makes an effort to understand his wife's physical needs. That is utterly practical and Paul is equally practical at the same level.

There are those that think Christian marriage will go along fine as long as spiritually everything is right, but that is not so. The spiritual side can go wrong as the result of the physical side going wrong. Therefore Peter is referring to consideration at the physical level, thoughtfulness, understanding, patience. Cruelty is often not deliberate but thoughtless. Marriages have been broken by thoughtlessness rather than deliberate cruelty.

The second thing is courtesy, which has been defined as love in little things. I think every one of us who is a husband would be a little embarrassed to compare the courtesies we extended in our courtship to the courtesies we extend now. Here the Word of God strikes deep. Chivalry should not be dead in Christian circles.

The thing that is good about what used to be called the women's liberation movement is that as far as I understand it, women are saying, "We are no longer things, we want to be people. We are not going to be treated as objects, we want to be subjects." This, I think, is what they are trying to say and that is good. But they are then going on to say something that is not right. They are then going on to use this term "equality" in the wrong way. God's Word says utterly, plainly: "Give courtesy to the woman as to the weaker sex." Those who defy that phrase are going against reality. I want to define what I believe is meant by the word "weaker" here, which makes courtesy and chivalry necessary. I believe that the word, "weaker" here means that a woman is more easily hurt physically, emotionally and mentally. It is for those three reasons that men are called to extend courtesy.

I don't know if you know why the bride always walks on the bridegroom's left arm. She actually comes into church on her father's right arm, but that is simply convenience. But she always goes out on her bridegroom's left arm, why? It is assuming that he is right-handed and that his fist or sword arm is free. If he is left-handed, she had better come around the other side. But this is the chivalry that says, my man can pull his sword out and fight for me. That is why we do it. It survives as a token of courtesy and is very rarely necessary today, but that's the reason behind it. Here is Peter saying, that courtesy is due for this reason and therefore there is a protection needed.

A well-known commentator said this about Genesis 3, the verse where it says God took a rib from Adam and made Eve: "He took woman from under man's arm that she might be protected, from his side that she might stand by his side, and from near his heart that she might be loved." That is a lovely comment. I think it shows an understanding of the way God meant us to live. Never does the Bible say that women are the inferior sex. The Bible never even suggests that and it is wrong thinking, for neither of us is inferior or superior, we are children of God. But we recognise the difference that God has placed, and we do not do as many people today are doing, seeking to obliterate the difference that the Creator has put in the creation and trying to turn creation as male into female and into something we call unisex.

Why should husbands have this attitude? There are two reasons and the first is inheritance. You are both going to inherit an eternal glory. In other words, in the next world there will not be this difference. In heaven, sex plays no part. They neither marry nor are given in marriage. In heaven we shall simply be the same before God, brother and sister if you like, in the family of God.

Peter is really saying that in view of the fact that you will both inherit an identical future, you have responsibilities to each other down here – not rights – since you are joint heirs and you are both going to come into everything God has for you. There is no inequality in God's sight, and this is where we get the foundation of feminine emancipation. Jesus looked at men and women and knew that both are sinners and he can get both to heaven as saints. That puts us on the same footing exactly.

Therefore, in Christ, at that point, there is neither male nor female. Looking into heaven, we see a joint inheritance. So whatever a man or a woman contribute to the marriage on earth, whether he brings money into the marriage or she brings money, whether it is her house or his (I hope it is theirs, that you have things jointly) you are all going to have the same kind of room up there and God will treat you exactly the same there.

The other reason – and here is a devastating thing – Peter is teaching that if your attitude to your wife is not right, don't expect your prayers to be answered. Somebody has put it this way most poignantly: "The sighs of an injured wife come between a husband's prayers and God's hearing." So let no husband think if he is treating his wife badly that he can do that and pray to God and have a prayer answered – God will say: "I'm deaf in that ear until your wife tells me that you are courteous and considerate."

Well this is the heart of marriage, and the difference between success and failure in marriage in God's sight is whether we achieve this kind of pattern. If you achieve this pattern, then I believe your children will be secure and happy. They will grow up to believe that they too can have a wonderful marriage. They will grow up to say, "I want a

Christian marriage too." This then is God's pattern. How can we be surprised when, having departed so far from God's ordained relationship between men and women, so many things go wrong, when marriages break up and children are left frightened and insecure? How can we doubt that God knows what he is doing when he tells us how we are to behave?

6

INNOVATION

Read 1 Peter 3:8–4:6

A. NEW RELATIONSHIPS (3:8–16)

    1. To insiders (8–12)
        a. What?
            i. United; ii. Sympathetic; iii. Loving;
            iv. Tender; v. Forgiving
        b. Why?
            i. God calling; ii. Own blessing
    2. To outsiders (13–16)
        a. What they do for us
            i. Can't be harmed; ii. Will be blessed;
            iii. Needn't be afraid
        b. What they say about us
            i. Mental defence; ii. Moral defence

B. NEW REFLECTIONS (3:18–4:6)

    1. Christian belief (18–19, 21–22)
        a. His death; b. His descent; c. His resurrection
        d. His ascension; e. Judgment
    2. Christian baptism (20–21)
        a. Christ and Noah
        b. Noah and Christians
    3. Christian behaviour (1–6)
        a. Have suffered
        b. Will suffer

God saves you into a family. Before you become Christ's, you
may have friends, you may have relatives, but before God you are all alone – and you will stand alone before him all alone one day. But when you become a Christian you have come into a family and you are part of a brotherhood that stretches over the whole world and even beyond this world into the next. Learning to live within that family is part of what God has called you to.

You may have heard of Schopenhauer's Parable of the Hedgehogs. A group of hedgehogs were cold in the winter so they huddled together underneath a tree root to get each other warm. But they pricked each other so they decided that it was better to be separated. They went out into the winter cold and they got very cold and they shivered. So they decided to try and have fellowship again. So they came together again and they prickled each other. So they set off again on their own and then they came together and they set off and it goes on and on this story. I am afraid it is the story of the Christian church for the last two thousand years. For one of the hardest things in the Christian life is getting on with other Christians. That is an honest thing to say but I want you to know it to be true. The reason is that you are called to live in a closer relationship with other people than you have ever lived before outside the circles that you choose and the circles of people you like. When you become Christ's, you are suddenly put together with people you would never otherwise have met. In Christ we are brothers and sisters and we are not perfect yet. The closer you come to each other, the more you see each other's faults. The nearer you get into the fellowship of a church, the more you will find out that your faith needs to be in Jesus rather than in Christians. But part of his salvation purpose is to prove to the world that people who otherwise would never have liked each other can love each other. We are people who have awkward corners still to be rubbed off, people with completely different temperaments and personalities – some of us could hardly be any more different in temperament and in many other ways, yet we have been called to live together as a family and that is God's purpose for us. Not to be individual Christians but to live together, to be the church of Jesus Christ which is why, as Peter goes through this letter, after thirty years of living for the Lord and preaching for the Lord and fighting for the Lord and suffering for the Lord, he is saying: finally I want to tell you how to get on with each other. He had no illusions and he was speaking straight to us Christians – with all our different temperaments, with all our different ideas and outlooks and backgrounds and hopes and dreams and fears and sorrows. For the one thing that will convince the world that we really are disciples of Jesus, really following him, is: "By this shall all men know that you are my disciples, that you love one another."

After Jesus called twelve men to follow him they were so different from each other that they were pretty soon arguing, fighting for the chief place in the kingdom and falling out with each other. Peter had asked, "How often shall my brother sin against me and I forgive him?" You notice he didn't put it the other way around: how often shall I sin against him and he forgive me? People following Christ have to live together.

Look at what Peter is saying here. Here is the most intimate relationship you can ever have. As soon as you become a Christian you feel closer to other Christians than to your own unsaved relatives; you feel you belong. You feel that Christians are real people and you always thought they were hypocrites. You feel that these are the people that you belong to and that you want to know better. But then you discover they are still on the road of holiness as you are. That can be a bit of a shock at first. Just remember that the nearer you come to Jesus, the worse the things you will discover about yourself too, and other people are having problems getting on with you as well as you with them.

Our relationships then, when we come into the family of God, are related to inside the church and outside the church. Peter has talked about our relationships with the government. When you become a Christian you have a new relationship with the government of your country. You are a citizen in a double sense. He has talked about your relationship with your employer—when you become a Christian you have a new relationship with your boss. He has talked about your relationships within the family. When you become a Christian you have a new relationship with your wife or your husband. Now he is teaching when you become a Christian you have got a new relationship with Christians, and that has got to be worked out.

Now he gives six characteristics of true family life in the church. Kenneth Taylor translates the first part of this passage like this: be as one big family. The pattern of the church's life together is the pattern of a family – not a lot of little cliques, not a lot of little meetings, not a lot of little clubs, but one big family.

Firstly, a true family is a *united* family. A divided family is an offence, there is something wrong with it. We have all said things to our own family that we should not have said. Be of one mind – now you notice the kind of unity God's family is supposed to have. It is not an organisational unity, not a visible thing, it is invisible. It is thinking the same way, having the same mind, the same outlook, sharing the same understanding so that there is one mind. Whose mind is it going to be? The minister's? No, it is going to be the mind of Jesus, one big family with one mind. Ideally, no church meeting ought ever to be other than unanimous on any issue. You are one big family with the same mind, the mind of Christ and he knows what is right. Therefore, the church should have one mind as to what is right. Be united.

Secondly, a true family is *sympathetic*. The word literally means to *suffer* with. If your child suffers, you suffer. If your partner suffers, you suffer. That is family life. If your children come home thrilled, you are thrilled. If one rejoices, all rejoice. If one weeps, all weep. That is family life – sympathy. Peter is encouraging believers to be one big, happy family as a church, so that if one is weeping the others weep, and if one is happy and rejoicing in the Lord the others shout "Hallelujah" too.

Thirdly, a true family is *loving*. That should go without saying. Family love is one of the loveliest things in the world. Notice that it doesn't say "liking". If the church is made up of those who like each other, then quite frankly it will be a church of a particular kind of people and no more. It would be just one big club or clique of people who like each other. Peter is talking about loving each other. It may even be that at first you might not like some of God's children, but you can start loving them straight away. You can love someone you don't like, and after a bit you find that loving them causes you to like them and you become one big family. How do you love them? You care for them, you pray for them, you talk to them, you mix with them – that is how you love. Love is primarily not what you *feel* but what you *do*. So we are to love and be a loving family, mutually caring for each other.

Fourthly, a family is to be *tender* according to Peter. Now that means to be sensitive. Is it not true that in a genuine family circle if someone has inner thoughts that they don't share with anybody else, thoughts that are troubling them, the rest of the family is sensitive; they know. It is apparent at the breakfast table. Nothing may be said but you are sensitive, you are tender, and you know something is wrong. I come down one morning and I look at my breakfast table and there is an envelope without a stamp or an address and I think: "What on earth is that and who has put that there?" I open it. It is a wedding anniversary card. Sensitive.... Well, in a true family there is sensitivity so that you know what the other is thinking even though they don't say it.

Fifthly, in a true family there has got to be *humility*. It is one of the most interesting facts about the ancient world that if you called a Greek person humble two thousand years ago they would have felt insulted because it meant then someone who grovelled. Jesus came into the world, took a grovelling word and he made it one of the greatest virtues. He said, "Learn of me for I am meek and lowly." In a true family there is not boasting. You don't boast in a family. If you try you will soon get knocked down to size. There is humility in a true family, lowliness.

Sixthly, the last thing Peter says you will have in a true family is *forgiveness*. You don't write off a member of a family permanently, you seek to forgive. That is where Peter, with a rather humorous memory says "Forgiving one another". He is remembering the day that he said to Jesus, "How often do I have to put up with this brother of mine?" It was Andrew. How often does he have to sin against me and I forgive him? "Seven," he thought. That was really pushing his forgiveness a long way! Seven times I forgive my brother. I think Andrew had just upset him for the eighth time and Peter was asking whether he could have a go at him then. The Lord's answer meant: Peter, stop counting. You don't count up things in a true family. It is sad when one counsels a couple who have fallen out with each other. One of them brings up things that were said twenty years ago, saying, "He said to me, and I said to him...." They go through a conversation from all that time ago. They can remember it all. They have been counting it all. In a true family you don't count up. You don't hold things against a person. You forgive.

If I describe a church that is the opposite of these six things, you would shudder. Imagine a church that is divided, selfish, careless, hard, proud, and malicious. Would you like to belong to a church like that? Well then, if you wouldn't like to belong to a church like that, seek to make your church what it ought to be. If ever you find a perfect church don't join it, you will spoil it. Now why should we have this kind of church? For two reasons. First of all it is our calling. God called us to live like this. He didn't just call us to enjoy him by ourselves. He called us to live together.

You see, the relationship I have with other Christians is different from every other relationship with anybody else for one reason. This is that it is a relationship which is going to go on forever. I am going to live with my fellow Christians forever. Every other human relationship will come to an end. Some of them I can end more quickly than others. But if I am related to a Christian, I'm going to live with them in glory forever. So it is our calling to live together on earth as those who are going to live together in heaven.

It is not only our calling, says Peter, it is our blessing. He quotes from Psalm 34, which promises good days. Do you want to live in good days? Then be in a church that is loving and tender and kind. I get very sad when I go to a church and people say, "Ah, they were good days." They are looking back to some past period in the church's life. I want to be in the kind of church that says, "These days are good days." It is wonderful to be in such a family. It is a blessing. God rewards those who live like this. His ear is open to their prayer. He listens to prayers of people living together in one big family and he blesses. So it is our calling and our blessing.

The last few verses in this passage talk about our relationship to those outside the family of God. When you become a Christian you not only become differently related to those inside the church, you will also become differently related to those outside. It is one of the sad consequences of following the Christian life that those who were formerly your friends don't like the change. I don't know if you had this experience. I think most people do. Those who were in the past glad to meet you and to mix with you are suddenly pulling away. You have to learn a new relationship to them too. It comes as a surprise to us. We want the world to know. We feel sure they would all be thrilled and waiting for the good news – I have found love and joy and peace and I am set free. Then we get an awful shock: Christ said that they hated him. He didn't promise us a picnic but a battle in which we would suffer. If any man will come after me it will be a daily cross. What do you do when you suffer? A lot of it will be unjust. Things will be done to you and said about you that are not deserved. What do you do with what they do to you? You remember three things that Peter said. He says you can't be harmed, you will be blessed, and you needn't be afraid. Next time you are suffering unjustly, just say to yourself—I can't be harmed, I will be blessed, and I need not be afraid because God says so. You can't be harmed. Jesus says don't be afraid of those that can kill your body and do nothing worse than that. What a way to talk! Surely they can't do any worse than kill your body, can they? Fear him who can destroy body and soul in hell. But even if they kill your body what have they done? They have got you to heaven sooner; they have got you to glory sooner. They helped you not hindered you. You can't be harmed. The life that God has given to you can't be touched. They can touch you physically but they can't touch you spiritually.

You will be blessed, because there is a blessing in being persecuted. Whenever I meet people who have suffered for their faith, do you know I envy them? The blessing it has given. They rejoice that they are worthy to suffer, and you need not be afraid because God will be there right with you, so why be afraid? What they say about us – how do you deal with that? You must have a double defence: a mental defence and a moral defence. Your mental defence is that you must be ready at any time to give a reason concerning your hope. The word "hope" is a bit of a wishy-washy word in English. It means I'm not quite sure. Is it going to be sunny on Monday? I hope so. That is the kind of word it has become. We think of the word "hope" as a kind of uncertain word meaning, "I wish, but I'm not sure." But the word "hope" in the Bible means I am absolutely sure. Your hope is an anchor, and an anchor is something pretty solid, and when it is locked on the rock, you have got something certain.

Isn't it lovely the way that God has used people to bring us the whole truth? Paul brought us the truth of faith; the apostle John brings to us the truth about love, but the favourite word of Simon Peter is *hope*, because Simon had become a rock and he was certain now. Peter's message is: when anybody tackles you and criticises you, be ready to tell them why you are sure, the reason for the certain hope that is in you. Be ready to give them a reason – that is your mental defence. It means you have got to do a bit of thinking about your faith.

You have got to be ready to say why you are sure. It means studying your Bible to be a workman who is not ashamed, handling rightly the word of truth. It means being ready to talk to people about your hope – so be ready. There must be a moral defence too. Whatever they say about you—and they will say outrageous things, the best defence is a clear conscience. If you have that, they can say what they like and it doesn't hurt because you know that God knows it's not true. So your new relationships as a Christian with those inside the church and with those outside the church are being formed in Christ.

*****

Peter wrote in his second letter, "Our beloved Paul spoke of this in his letters. There are some things in them hard to understand." But here Peter gives us the most difficult passage in the New Testament in his own letter. There are many things in this little passage which are very difficult for us to understand. For example, the mention of Christ preaching to the spirits in prison has puzzled a lot of people. Who were they? Where were they? Then again, there is this business about baptism now saves you. That's a very strong, high view of baptism. It's a view that some Baptists have difficulty with. Baptism now saves you. Does that mean if I am not baptised I am not saved? Then there is the problem of that little phrase in 4:1, "Whoever has suffered in the flesh has ceased from sin." What does that mean? Does it mean that if I have suffered physically, I am perfect spiritually?

The advantage of going straight through a letter is you have got to tackle the difficulties and you can't jump over them and give out another text. There are certain principles of understanding the Bible. The first is that you will never really get the truth of the Bible unless you are prepared not only to read it but to study it. The Bible itself tells you to study: to show yourselves approved to God, handling aright the word of truth. Peter at the beginning of this very letter has said "Gird up your minds" – which in modern English would be: "Tighten the belt of your minds; roll the sleeves of your mind up." In other words, get down to a bit of thinking! You will never understand the Bible until you learn to really dig and think. A second rule for understanding the Bible is to take the Bible in its plainest, simplest meaning even if it seems a bit strange to you. Don't try and twist the words around; don't try and look for some hidden meaning. Just take the words at first in the plainest, simplest meaning and see where that leads you.

Rule number three is to look at the *context*. That means that if you have a verse or a text you don't understand, look at the verses in front of it and the verses after it. Look at the chapter it is in, look at the book it is in and say, "What's all this bit about? What subject is he talking about?" Then you'll understand the text. A fourth rule is: never use one text to contradict a lot of others.

Using these simple rules I have tried to look at these passages. The first thing I notice is that in v. 15 we are told that Peter is writing to those who are suffering. The whole background to this letter is precisely that this letter is for those who suffer for their faith. I am not suffering for my faith at the moment. One reason we don't understand this letter too easily can be because we are not suffering. People who are paying the price for being Christians today read this letter and it speaks to their condition; they understand what it is all about. In v. 17 Peter is talking about a particular kind of suffering. First it is *undeserved* suffering, which is one of the most difficult kinds of suffering to bear. If you have deserved it and you are paying the bill for playing the fool then you can face it. But when you haven't done anything to deserve it and particularly, when you have done good and done right and you suffer for it, that is not easy.

Secondly, it is *ordained* suffering; suffering that God wills you to go through. Some of the suffering that we Christians have, we have caused ourselves. It was not God's will, we were just awkward people, silly people, stiff-necked people, and we must not then say that that is suffering in God's will – we caused it. But God wills that his people should suffer sometimes. So we are talking about undeserved suffering, ordained suffering, and thirdly we are talking about *physical* suffering; suffering in the flesh.

I remember a little proverb that used to be quoted to me: sticks and stones hurt your bones but names don't hurt at all – and I don't think that is strictly true. When people call you things that are undeserved it can hurt but not so much as when you are going through it physically. If you read the story of Pastor Richard Wurmbrand, for example, of his physical sufferings – I wonder how many of us could go through that. We would need a lot of grace to stand the physical suffering.

Peter was writing to those who were going to be burned alive, thrown to the lions, tortured for their faith, and it is that background that lies behind all these passages. The key words in this passage are *flesh* and *spirit*. Again and again through the passage Peter talks about "in the flesh", "in the spirit". In modern English: physical; spiritual. What he is saying all the way through this passage is: when you go through it physically, don't just stop there in your thinking. Ask what is going to result spiritually from the physical suffering. Many have found that physical suffering can bring great spiritual blessing. In the amazing ways of God, the things that the world would count tragedies can become triumphs in God.

What Peter is going to say to those who suffer physically is this: look what can happen spiritually. It is not what they do to your body that matters, it is what is going to happen to your spirit as a result, and that can be wonderful. Everything he says about Christ speaking to the spirits in prison, about baptism saving you, about those who have suffered in the flesh having ceased from sin, are tied together on this one thread. What happens to you physically will have a spiritual effect. That applied to Jesus, it applied to Noah, it applies to those who have been baptised, and it applies to those who suffer for the faith. What happens to them physically will have a spiritual effect.

Take first of all the suffering of Jesus—the greatest example of undeserved suffering there has ever been. The just man, the righteous man, the good man, the perfect man, and at the age of thirty-three he went through the most horrible suffering. What is crucifixion really? It is to be stripped naked, flogged to within an inch of your life, nailed to a block of wood without anaesthetic, strung up and exposed to the heat of the midday sun, your body gradually being dehydrated until your mouth is absolutely dry and you are thirsty. You can only breathe by holding yourself up on your feet on the nails through your feet, and because of the pain that causes your body to sag, and then you get congestion of the lungs and you suffocate. Alternately, you force yourself to breathe at the cost of pain and then suffocate and it goes on like that for hours and maybe even days. Jesus suffered. It was totally undeserved but it was ordained. It was the will of God that he should suffer.

Now think of this: that physical suffering has brought spiritual salvation to millions. Look at the spiritual effect of the physical suffering of Jesus. He died on the cross, the just for the unjust, to bring us to God and the result is that millions now know God because he suffered physically. When you are going through physical suffering for the Lord, if ever you are called upon to tread this way, bear in mind what God did with the suffering of Jesus, and you will say, "What can he do with mine?" Look what he has done with the suffering of so many martyrs already, who have inspired many other Christians to put their faith in Almighty God.

This then is the first illustration of Jesus dying: his physical agony produced for us spiritual atonement with God. So physical suffering can be used for spiritual good.

So far we can understand it perfectly well, but now we go from his dying to his death. To all human appearances that was the end of Jesus' ministry. I can imagine that those who buried Jesus, wrapping that body in the bandages, looking at that cold, grave face with the eyes closed, must have thought those lips could never again speak the truth, those eyes never again look with compassion on people, those frozen hands never again touch the sick. But they were wrong. Do you know that while they were burying his body, Jesus was preaching? That is what Peter says now.

It may be a thought that you have never had before. I am not now referring to his resurrection. That happened three days later. I am referring to the day that Jesus died. While they conducted the funeral and put Jesus' body in the ground, Jesus was preaching. You can't stop Jesus. His physical death led to a spiritual ministry. It is enshrined in the Apostles' Creed – "He descended into Hades." What did he do when he got there? What do you imagine Jesus would do? Wherever he was, he preached, and he preached the good news. Here is an amazing revelation in the Scripture – it is right here that when Jesus actually came to death physically but spiritually he carried right on. Of course, his death removed him from this world for three days but it just put him into another world. The word "Hades" simply means where the spirits of the departed wait for judgment day. Jesus, the Son of God, was now put right into a place he had not been before. So he was able to preach during those three days he was there, before his spirit and his body were reunited on Easter Sunday morning. You can't stop Jesus preaching the good news. So he was put to death in the flesh but he was made alive in the Spirit. What a comfort to those who are in danger of being put to death in the flesh, to know that even though their body may be killed, that doesn't finish them; that doesn't finish their conscious experience. That doesn't finish their activity – far from it. Jesus was put to death in the flesh, made alive in the Spirit. No wonder he said to his disciples, "Don't be afraid of those who kill your body". They can do nothing more, they can't stop you.

I think we ought to get thoroughly adjusted to death in this way. A dead body is no more than someone's old overcoat. It doesn't stop them. You may bury the body they have used and lived in, but they are no longer in it. The spirit is free and alive and this is how the Bible teaches us to think. If you think at the human level, you will think that between his death and resurrection Jesus did nothing. You will think of him as a dead body lying in a tomb and you are thinking quite wrongly. That body of Jesus was just the house he had lived in for thirty-three years. Jesus was busy preaching between the day he died and Easter Sunday morning. This is what Peter is talking about here. What a comfort to those who think that death would be the end of everything. It wasn't with Jesus; it won't be with you.

Once again, a physical tragedy becomes a spiritual triumph. Once again, what happens to the body has a spiritual effect that is beneficial, setting you free to do something else. Can you see how Peter's mind is working? Don't worry about physical suffering, think of the spiritual benefits. So he moves on: where did Jesus preach during those three days and to whom was he preaching? Now we come to the point that he was alive in the spirit even though he was dead in the flesh, and in the live spirit that he had, he went and preached to the spirits in prison. We are given one further clue that they had some connection with the days of Noah. Now I am quite sure you know the story of Noah and his ark. There was a wonderful cantata about it which is very dramatic, particularly when the floods come and you hear the people singing but crying, "Oh God forgive me." Do you realise that they were crying too late? That actually happened. Noah's flood is a historical event and God did it. Some of the people involved in the flood are those referred to by this phrase "the spirits in prison".

There are two possible answers to the question as to who they were. One I will just mention but not go into in detail because it doesn't convince me, namely that the spirits referred to were the angels who in Noah's day made earthly women pregnant. There was some kind of horrible alliance between spirits and people in those days. It was one of the reasons why God wiped out the world with a flood. It was a horrible thing that was happening. Those who say it was angels refer to 2 Peter and Jude, concerning angels who left their proper place and are now being kept in custody by God until the judgment day. It may refer to them. But I am afraid I am not convinced because the group here described are those who were disobedient when God was patiently waiting for them in the days of Noah, while he built his ark. Who could that refer to? I think the answer is very simple: those who knew Noah was building an ark but wouldn't go into it, those for whom God waited a hundred and twenty years for them to come into the ark. While Noah and his sons were building this raft, God, through Noah, preached to everybody. They laughed at him, but Noah went on building and he told the people that God was going to destroy the world. They could be saved if they would believe, obey and go in. God waited, but only seven people believed Noah and the rest did not obey and were drowned. Their bodies and spirits were separated by the floodwater. Their bodies were rotting in the floodwater but their spirits did not end. Their spirits were kept in custody in prison until the judgment day. Jesus went and preached to them. Between his death and resurrection, he went to those, in a sense, whose judgment day had come before their time, whose lives had been cut short by God; and God has not done it since. He has made a promise, and he has never again destroyed society since then. Not until the end of the earth will he do it.

So Jesus went to those who came under that severe judgment of God – those who were made an example of God's justice to every subsequent age – and he gave them another chance. How like God to think of those whose opportunity he had cut short. Jesus went and preached to them. We can therefore say about these obstinate people who refused to believe that what happened to them physically turned out for their spiritual good. They were physically made an example of God's judgment and physically they were drowned. Therefore spiritually they got a chance to hear the gospel from the lips of Jesus. Once again the physical tragedy became a spiritual triumph – do you see it? You find it mentioned again at 4:6. You see once again flesh – judged; spirit – quickened. The same theme goes on through.

The same thing may be said of Noah. He went into the ark having built it and for over a year lived in the very uncomfortable quarters with his animals. I am quite sure that he was worried about the rain and whether the craft would survive – though God had told him how to build it and God doesn't design things badly. He knew that the water that was drowning others was saving him. The water that was covering others was lifting him up, and through the water he was saved. He was saved physically but the physical thing that happened to Noah; the physical act of going through the ark, through the waters, and coming into a new, clean world, led to his spiritual salvation because we are told in Hebrews that by faith Noah went into the ark and this brought him the righteousness that is by faith. Once again the theme is that a physical act leads to spiritual blessing.

Peter explains that baptism is exactly the same kind of experience. You go through the waters, and it is a physical act, it happens to your body, but look what happens to you spiritually as a result. Baptism corresponds to Noah's flood. When you are buried in the waters of baptism, you are in a situation of drowning. You are going through your flood but like Noah you come out all right. More than that, the physical act of going through the water and coming through that experience does something to you spiritually. I take quite literally in its simplest sense the phrase "baptism now saves you." I don't believe it is just a symbol. I don't believe it is a public testimony or confession of faith. It is difficult to prove that from the Bible and I would baptise somebody in water if there was nobody there to watch. It is nice to share it but it is not primarily a testimony. It is not primarily a symbol of something that has already happened. Baptism now saves you. It is part of God's salvation.

So that no-one jumps to wrong conclusions, let me say what I mean. Does that mean that somebody who has not been baptised is lost? No. I want you to notice that Jesus said, "He who believes and is baptised is saved." He put the two things together: believing and being baptised. But then he said, "He who believes not is condemned." A person is not condemned for not being baptised but for not believing. But if a man is saved it is through believing and being baptised. What does the word "saved" mean here? If we are not careful, we tend to use the word to mean only to be saved from the guilt of sin and the punishment of hell. But the Bible means much more than that. It means not only to be saved from the guilt of sin and the punishment of sin in the future; it means to be saved from the power of sin in the present. He says, "Baptism saves us now." We are not now discussing your salvation in the future when you face the judgment seat of God, we are talking about sin now. Baptism is to save you now. It is God's way of getting you clean now. It was God's way of washing Noah's dirty, old world out of existence and putting him in a clean world to go through the waters of the flood. It is God's way of saving you now – to take you through the waters and to wash away that old world of yours and to put you in a clean life. So Peter is pointing to the fact that baptism, although it is a physical act, has spiritual results. It is not the washing of dirt from the body. It is an appeal to God for a clean conscience. It is asking God to cleanse that little world in which you live. It is the world inside because the real world in which you live is the world inside. If that is wrong, the world outside will be too. You are saying: "God, destroy my world in the flood and bring me safely through to a new world." That is what you are doing; you are appealing to God for a clear conscience. The physical act of baptism saves you now. It is part of God's present salvation from the power of sin and from the dirt of sin. Once again Peter is saying that what happens to you physically has spiritual effects even in your baptism.

How does this work? How can it actually cleanse a person? There is nothing magic in the water or in the people baptising. Peter says "by the resurrection of Jesus" – because Jesus is alive, baptism now saves you. Here and now in this life, it helps you to be clean, helps you to live in a new world because Jesus is alive. Whenever we baptise people, Jesus is standing in the water with us. You are buried with him in baptism, you are raised with him to walk in a new life. It is actually happening now because Jesus is alive and because he is not only risen but ascended at the right hand of God.

Every power and authority and spirit is under his control and therefore he can guarantee you that new world. You are being baptised into his death, his burial and his resurrection. Jesus will bring you through, like Noah, from an old world that you lived in to a new world. Baptism is his chosen way of doing it – a physical act that brings spiritual benefit.

Something often follows baptism – a Christian gets buffeted, tossed about. The thing is that when you come out into that new world, the other side of the flood, you are different. Your old pals are puzzled, your old friends do not understand why you can't join in the things that you did with them. You are living in a new world now, a washed world, a cleansed world, and your old friends won't understand what has happened. Social ostracism follows.

We can understand from what Peter writes that before you went through the flood, there was an old world that you were living in, which was doing what others like to do. You were joining them in all the activities they liked, living it up, just doing what everybody does, doing as the Gentiles do. He lists all kinds of "party activities" – living for kicks, doing what the Gentiles do. But now you have come out into a new world and you have spent enough of your life on what others want you to do. For the rest of your time you are going to spend it on what God wants you to do. You now ask: what does God like me to do? Now you are going to live that way and the result is you are going to suffer. If you're at school, you will suffer at school. If you are in a home where there are people who are not Christian, you are going to suffer at home. If you are at work with people who aren't Christians, you will suffer there. "Whoever would live a godly life in Christ Jesus shall suffer persecution." John Bunyan, who spent twelve years in jail because he was a nonconformist, put that text at the head of his autobiography *Grace Abounding to the Chief of Sinners*, subtitled: "Whoever would live a godly life in Christ Jesus shall be persecuted." There was a day when John Bunyan was a hard drinking, hard gambling, swearing young man in Bedford and he did what the Gentiles did. He had a name through the district for being a leader of the bad guys in that area. But one day, walking home through the streets of the town, he heard a group of housewives gossiping in a backyard. They were talking about Jesus, and this hard living young man listened to that over the fence and something stirred in his heart. He found Jesus and he was baptised and the flood washed away his old world and he went to jail for twelve years. He had to leave behind his wife and his little blind child. But the spiritual benefit to the world is *The Pilgrim's Progress*. Once again, the physical act brought a spiritual benefit. You see, you cannot separate flesh and spirit while you are in this world – what happens to one will affect the other. Flesh and spirit affect each other and that can be turned to your advantage.

So when you suffer and when your old friends begin to call you names, and when they do worse than that, then let me tell you this: they will answer to God; they must give account to him who judges the living and the dead. You don't need to take any revenge. You don't need to answer back. God says, "Vengeance is mine, I will repay." One day they will stand before God and God will say, "You laughed at me and you called me names," and they will say, "When did we laugh at you, when did we call you names?" He will say as much as you did it to the least of these my brethren you did it to me. "Saul, Saul, why do you persecute me?" What you do to Christians you do to Christ. So you can leave them in his hands. But what about yourself? The physical suffering that you have will bring spiritual blessing.

We come to the last problem in this passage: what is meant by the phrase, "Whoever has suffered in the flesh has ceased from sin"? Is the phrase "ceased from sin" the cause of the suffering or the effect of the suffering? Some people feel that it means that it is the cause. In other words, the fact that you ceased from sin led to your suffering; the fact that you stopped doing wrong things led to persecution. There is a truth in that, but the grammar here does not quite fit that interpretation. The grammar points to the other conclusion and it is a thrilling one. Kenneth Taylor translates it like this, I think perfectly: "when your body suffers, sin loses its power". What a promise! If you suffer physically for the Lord, you will discover that the physical passions of the flesh, which were a problem to you before, cease to be so. What a lovely promise. Wouldn't that make you almost eager to suffer? To think that that benefit would come – and yet there it is stated that those who suffer for the Lord find sin less of a problem. I think it is one of the divine compensations that only God could think up: that when you suffer for him, he will make the fight with yourself that much easier. So physical suffering can bring spiritual holiness and those who have suffered physically for the Lord have found this to be true.

Peter is teaching us to arm ourselves with this thought. We are to get ready for the battle. I do not know when physical suffering is going to come to England. I don't think it's far off because the law of violence is now spreading through the land. There is coming a day, and it may not be many years hence, when people will be frightened to come to Christian meetings at night for fear of being waylaid. It is already true in parts of England that midweek meetings are suffering in church life because people are frightened to be accosted on the way home. Arm yourselves with this thought: those who suffer cease from sin. Maybe that is why we don't show holiness so much, for the opposite is true. The more physical comfort and ease you have, the more you indulge yourself.

Do you notice that in dealing with this question of suffering in the flesh and benefitting in the Spirit, Peter talks about Jesus all the way? The Apostles' Creed is a summary of what he said. It was not written until a century or so later but it goes back to Peter's teaching. Consider the middle section of that creed. It is about Jesus: "He suffered under

Pontius Pilate, was crucified, dead, and buried. He descended into Hades; the third day he rose again from the dead; he ascended into heaven, and sitteth on the right hand of God the Father Almighty; from thence he shall come to judge the quick and the dead." The words of that creed are in this section of 1 Peter. When you are facing suffering, affirm the words of that creed. Are you ready to meet the one who is going to judge the quick and the dead? The people who were drowned in Noah's flood got a second chance the other side of the grave because Jesus preached the gospel to them and they were converted. But don't think that after your death – when your spirit and your flesh are separated and your flesh rots in the grave or is burned in the crematorium, and your spirit survives – don't think that Jesus will come and preach to your spirit, because he is not in Hades now. He was only there for the three days.

There have been those who built on this passage of Peter what has been called the "gospel of the second chance". You cannot build that doctrine on this verse. What we have to say is: *now* is the day of salvation. We have heard the gospel and he is going to judge the living and the dead.

7

CONSUMMATION

Read 1 Peter 4:7–11

A. THE REVELATION FROM GOD (7a)
  1. The End is coming
  2. The End is near

B. THE REACTION OF MEN (7b–11)
  1. What to do with your *mind* (7b)
    a. Not panic
    b. But sane and sober
  2. What to do with your *heart* (8)
    a. Love deeply
    b. Love covers a multitude of sins
  3. What to do with your *home* (9)
    a. Hospitality to one another
    b. Without grumbling
  4. What to do with your *gifts* (10)
    a. Service
    b. Stewardship
  5. What to do with your *voice* (11)
    a. Words of God
    b. Praise of God

On 4th April 1912, the largest ship of her day, the Titanic, was steaming west on her maiden voyage at twenty-two knots in the north Atlantic, some five hundred miles southeast of Cape Race, Newfoundland. At 11:40 that night, in calm and clear weather, one of the lookouts notified the bridge that an iceberg lay right ahead. The first officer leapt to the engine room telegraph, rang it over to stop, and shouted, "Hard a' starboard" to the quartermaster at the wheel. (In those days, British merchant marine helm orders were given as though the ship's wheel was a tiller.) Probably the order was a mistake – one for which the officer paid with his life. But to have grasped the full consequence of his order at that moment would have required almost superhuman foresight.

Had the Titanic struck the iceberg head on, it is likely that her watertight compartments could have kept her afloat at least until the arrival of the Carpathia the following morning. Because the bow swung to the left in answer to the rudder, the ship struck a glancing blow. As she slowly ground past the iceberg, a deep projection of ice tore a gash three hundred feet long in her right side below the waterline. The wound opened six of the sixteen watertight compartments that were designed to make her unsinkable. When the sun rose the Titanic was on the bottom. Of her 2,224 people, 1,513 had been drowned. I want you to imagine that on board the Titanic when she set sail from England in 1912, there was a Christian with the gift of prophecy.

I want you to imagine that God had revealed to that prophet the fact that the ship would not reach America and was going to be sunk. I want you to try and imagine the attempts of a man who knew that to persuade people to prepare for what was going to happen. I can imagine him going to the crew of the ship, to the captain, and the rest of the crew and saying, "This ship is going to go down." I can imagine them saying, "It is unsinkable. The very finest brains of men have produced a ship that cannot sink." I can imagine him going to the passengers and saying, "This ship will not reach its destination" and the passengers saying, "Run away. We are enjoying ourselves." At the very moment when the ship struck the iceberg the passengers were engaged in a ball. They had eaten a lavish dinner and now they were dancing to music.

I can imagine that a man who went around saying that sort of thing on a ship would be regarded as a religious crank. As indeed anybody who wears a placard saying, "The end of all things is at hand" would be so treated today. Yet I have used this picture to try to convey to you the frustration of Christians who know that the world is going to end but nobody believes it. We know because God has revealed it by his prophets that this planet is not going to sail on forever. We know that the end of the world will come. The first words of the passage are: "The end of all things is at hand." Do you believe that? The world will consider you a religious crank if you do, but the Word of God teaches it.

Now we are going to ask the question: if we really believe that the end of all things is at hand, what difference will that make to our lives tomorrow or the next day? Will it cause us to do eccentric things? Will it cause us to panic? Can I put it this way: supposing you had been to the doctor this week and the doctor had said, "As far as I can see from your condition you have another six months to live" – knowing that the end was at hand, what would you do? Would you go off to work as usual tomorrow? Would you try to visit all the places you have long wanted to see? Would you start a hectic round of visits to relatives? The Bible teaches us to have this dimension of the end of all things being at hand to govern our daily life – to realise that the ship is going down.

Let us take the illustration of the Titanic one stage further. Supposing the prophet on board the ship said, "You could all be safe if you will take to the lifeboat now." Did you know that even after the Titanic struck the iceberg they couldn't persuade the passengers to take to the lifeboats? The ship stayed up for some time and it seemed so solid and so secure the passengers said, "No, we've been told this is unsinkable. This is the maiden voyage of the first unsinkable ship in the world." They had a job to persuade them to take to the little bobbing lifeboats on the Atlantic swell. The lifeboats looked so frail, so small, so insecure.

In the rest of this letter, Peter is speaking as a prophet and is saying: the world is sinking; it is going to go down; transfer to the church. The church is the lifeboat and yet the world seems so solid, so secure, and you feel it is there forever. The church to some seems so frail and so weak and so insecure. Yet God is saying through his Word: Unless you leave the world and transfer to the church of Jesus Christ, you will go down with the ship; the end of all things will be the end of you too. Now what difference does it make? Before we answer that question, let us just look at these two ideas that Peter is here predicting. Number one is that the world will come to an end; number two is that the end is at hand. Do we really believe those two things? Take the first prediction, that the world will come to an end. There have been many scientific debates about this. Some politicians seem to think that man will end the world. Others seem to think man will muddle through. But we make a fundamental mistake if we think this world is going to survive forever – or even the universe. It will not go on forever. God has revealed that it had a beginning and it will have an end. The

God who began it will be the God who will end it. Man will not end the world. God has said that it is in his hands, he is going to do it. He has not told us when. Thank God he hasn't, because if God had given us the date and it wasn't within our lifetime we wouldn't worry and if it was within our lifetime, we would panic.

But he has told us how and we know from the Word of God that he will bring it all to an end by reducing it to energy in fire. For two thousand years people have laughed at these statements in the Bible about the world ending in a gigantic fire, but we no longer laugh since we discovered what the atom was made of. Rutherford working in the Cambridge Laboratory, found out that the atom is a packed bonfire. We now know that to be true. We have seen the films of Hiroshima and Nagasaki. We know what there is packed in every atom – the energy that is there to be released.

One scientist said that if only one had the apparatus you could start a reaction in the universe that would in fact mean that the entire universe would dissolve in fire in forty minutes flat. But of course, there is no apparatus for man. There is no button that man can press that could do this, but God's finger is on the button. How far are we away from the end of the universe? The answer is forty minutes – or, to put it another way, how far are we away from the end of the world? – The length of God's finger. This is the atmosphere in which Christians ought to live. This is the background in which we ought to look at our daily life: that God's finger could touch that button whenever he chooses and end it all.

Do you realise that the sun only rose this morning because God willed that it should do so? It will only rise tomorrow morning if God agrees that it should. He is in charge of the entire universe. So the world is coming to an end, but what about this statement: the end of all things is at hand. Remember that the man who said that said it two thousand years ago. People have laughed at Peter (he knew they would). Did he think everything is coming to an end? They would say: everything has stayed the same since creation; there is nothing to worry about – it is there, it always will be there. It has been there another two thousand years.

Peter says, "Don't you realise that a thousand years is just like a day to God?" So it is only a couple of days since Peter said this – in God's timing – and God is very patient. What does it mean that it is at hand? It means precisely what I have said: that the hand of God is near the button. The phrase "at hand" is not so much a phrase of time as a phrase of space. It is near to God's finger and God could at any time end the whole thing. While the scientist says that it will take billions of years for this earth to cool down and become uninhabitable, God could say: I could end it tomorrow morning because I began it and I keep it going and I will end it.

What is our reaction to all that? Funnily enough, when the end comes, when the crisis is realised, when you have really believed that this is in fact the state of things, it changes your ideas. Something that happened on the Titanic when it went down was that a wealthy lady was seen running back from a lifeboat to her cabin. It was known that she had many jewels in that cabin and she had been wearing the jewels earlier at the ball, and she ran back and everybody thought she would run for her jewels, but when she came back she was carrying a paper bag with oranges in it. Somehow the crisis had changed her whole outlook. She now saw oranges as more useful than diamonds because there were going to be children in the lifeboat who needed liquid refreshment. If you realise the real situation of the world, it is bound to change your ideas. You will not become so attached to the things that are going to end, and you will become more attached to the things that are going to last. Does it mean that you are going to panic? Well, let's look at what Peter says. What is the reaction of Christians to the knowledge that the world could end whenever God decided; that the end of all things is at his hand? Well, there are four areas of life that Peter describes: what happens to your mind; what happens to your heart; what happens to your home, and what happens to your gifts. These are four most surprising things.

Incidentally, this provides the answer to what you should do if your doctor gives you six months to live because it is the same situation – the end is at hand. What do you do? Take the first thing: what happens to a Christian's *mind*? To the unbeliever, if he or she knew that the world might end any time, he would panic and two things would happen: he would lose his mental balance and he would lose his moral balance. He would tend to be in a turmoil of thoughts and he would tend to give way also to the things that his nature wanted to do because now there is a possibility of doing them and getting away with it.

According to Peter, a Christian will stay sane and sober. It is vital when there is a crisis of this kind and the end is at hand that people keep their heads. It was vital when the Titanic went down that the people manning the lifeboats stayed sane and sober. Some of the passengers were drunk and they were no use to other people, but the people who manned the lifeboats stayed sane and sober. They didn't panic; they kept cool; they kept their heads. So we are not to be drunk or frivolous or irresponsible, we will be needed by others; they will need to rely upon us. Do you realise that because the world is going to go, Christians are the one group of people who will be able to help to save souls and therefore we must keep cool. As we see the signs of the end approaching and you just need to read a single newspaper to see the signs of the crash coming, the Christian must keep sane and sober, even as he reads of wars and rumours of wars.

He will read of financial crises, natural disasters, famine and earthquake, but the Christian stays sane and sober. It is the only way that he can help other people. He doesn't panic; he doesn't rush around.

Peter says that it is essential that you stay sane and sober for your prayers. Your prayers are the first thing to reflect mental disturbance. Prayers can so easily be panic prayers and that is the kind of prayer that unbelievers pray—they pray to God but they are disturbed prayers, clutching at straws; they are panicking, so they pray. But a Christian knows he stays sane and sober for his prayers so that his prayer is calm, quiet and confident and he can pray for other people. The world will pray to God when the crunch comes – my how they will. Yes they will panic but the Christian will quietly pray.

Do you remember Peter in the garden of Gethsemane when the crisis was looming and there was a sense of impending doom settling on the disciples on that night? What did Jesus say to the panicking disciples? Watch and pray. As the end of all things gets nearer, and as we see it happening before our eyes, watch and pray. Keep your cool and pray.

The second thing is this: what do you do with your *heart*? The normal reaction to knowing that time is limited is to become self-centred, or even family-centred, to withdraw from a lot of relationships, to become more concerned with self or with immediate relatives. This is one of the natural reactions to a limited time.

But here we are told, as the end is at hand: let your love flow out even more. Make relationships and love one another. Make quite sure that you are not becoming self-centred through the crisis that is looming, that you are not getting wrapped up in a smaller group of people – but let your love flow out. Love one another, for love covers a multitude of sins. What does that mean? It certainly doesn't mean that you can atone for the sins of other people or your own. What it does mean is exactly what it says. That in that day love is prepared to reach out to others and cover their sins. In other words, there will be people who will be revealed as evil people in the crises, but love will cover that and still go on loving. Love will still see them as people who need salvation even though towards the end the worst in human nature will come out.

Love will be prepared to cover that for the sake of saving a person and love will go on. I notice by the way that it says love one another with special reference to Christians as if the team in the lifeboat must be closer and closer together if it is going to do its job. In a lifeboat, you must have teamwork in the stress and strain of saving folk. It is vital that, as the church draws nearer to the last days, Christians should love one another and cover a multitude of sins within the fellowship in order that they may save others.

What do you do with your *home*? Supposing you knew that your home was to be destroyed in six months or that your life was going to end in six months, what would you do with your house? Some people would close it down and just travel. Others would certainly stop decorating it or rebuilding bits of it. Well, what do you do with your home? The answer is because the end of the world is at hand, throw your home open with ungrudging hospitality to one another. In the last days of human history, the Christian home is going to be one of the vital factors in saving people. Churches may well be closed as we draw near to the end of all things but the Christian home becomes a little haven where people can come. They will turn to those who are sane and sober. There will be people who will want to find a little harbour where they can go to find a bit of peace in a world that is crashing around their ears. You see what practical implications this has. If you really believe that the end of the world is near, then your home will be thrown open to people this week because that is a Christian reaction.

Finally, what about your *gifts*? The natural reaction to the end of the world would be to stop using your gifts. "There is no time now for normal employment. Give up your job, give up your voluntary service. There's no point in doing anything now." That is how the unbeliever would argue, but the believer argues the opposite way. If the end of the world is near, I must use my gifts and serve my fellow men to the last ditch. We are to be sane, sober, getting on with the job right to the end. Jesus said, "Blessed are those servants who when the Lord comes he finds so doing." Because the end of the world is at hand we get on with the job he has given us to do so that when he comes we are busy doing it. Lord Shaftesbury did so much for the factories and the mines of our country, and had a concern for chimney sweep boys and pantomime children and anybody who was being exploited and abused, and every letter he wrote had at the head a text: "Even so, come Lord Jesus." The sense of the end of the world made him the useful citizen that he was. The sense that the end of all things was at hand made him use his gifts.

Now Peter gives an illustration of two gifts: a gift of word and a gift of deed. He refers to a preacher and then a deacon. (The word means someone who serves in a practical way.) He is teaching that if your job is preaching then you preach right to the end, because in the last minute you might save someone through the gospel. Go on preaching right to the last ditch – heaven and earth may pass away but his Word doesn't. To those whose gifts are giving practical help and service and administration: you go on doing that right to the end.

I believe God has given a gift to every believer, or he would if they would receive one. Never believe that you have no gifts to exercise. He could give you some and use them right to the end.

Why does the Christian react in this unusual way? Why does the Christian not panic but keep a sane and sober mind? Why does a Christian not get wrapped up in himself and his relatives but goes on loving? Why does a Christian not close his home down and go on his travels but open his home and say, "Come in"? Why does a Christian not say "It's no use now the end of the world is near?" No, a Christian says, "I'm going to work to the very end." Why?

For two reasons. First: though the end of all things is at hand, that is not the end of all people. Even though the universe is to go, people will go on. There is a heaven to enjoy and a hell to be endured beyond – and that is what makes it all worthwhile to go on loving and to go on serving and to go on inviting.

Second: the end of God will never come. So Peter finishes up with this phrase: "... that God may be glorified." Why are you here? What's the main purpose of life? Is it to enjoy yourself? To leave the world a little better than you find it? No! It is to glorify God; to live such a life that people give glory to God and say, "What a wonderful God his God must be." That is your purpose, and as you realise that this world is not here forever but will come to an end – the ship of the world is sinking – that is why your reaction is to go on serving and to go on loving and to go on inviting people into your home. So the end of all things is at hand, but we give glory to God forever.

8

OPPOSITION

Read 1 Peter 4:12–19

A. NOT SURPRISED (12)
      1. Usual
      2. Useful

B. NOT MISERABLE/DEPRESSED (13–14)
      1. Future
      2. Present

C. NOT ASHAMED (15–16)
      1. Not as criminals
      2. But as Christians

D. NOT RESENTFUL (17–18)
      1. Believer
      2. Unbeliever

E. NOT DISCOURAGED (19)
      1. Goodness
      2. God

I'll never forget the day that I met someone who had been in prison for Jesus and said, "I understand you've been in prison for Jesus." As soon as I said it I could have bitten my tongue out. His face creased up and he began to cry and said, "I wish not to speak." I thought of my foolishness. Just because I haven't known suffering myself I just didn't understand what it can mean, what after-effects it can have. Why did I have to bring it up?

When Peter wrote this letter he was writing in a situation where he knew that Christians were going to suffer. He was probably writing from Rome and probably writing during the reign of Nero, who for his own blunders was going to make Christians the scapegoat, and he was going to burn them alive, having dipped them in pitch. He was going to dress them in the skins of wild animals and throw them into the arena with real wild animals. He was going to crucify them. Peter realised that the ripples of this persecution would spread and reach the furthermost shores of the empire.

So he writes this to get Christians in Asia Minor ready for the ripples of this coming storm. This is now the fourth time in 1 Peter that we have had a passage on suffering. There is a paragraph in chapter 1 on suffering, there is a paragraph in chapter 2 and another in chapter 3. Here is one in chapter 4 and we shall find the same in chapter 5: You are going to suffer. How can you get ready for it?

There are five pieces of advice for when suffering hits you here in this short paragraph. Notice that Peter writes this before suffering had reached them. It may be fairly soon in this country when Christians suffer more. Therefore, it is good for us to be ready and to learn how to approach it. Here is the first of the five points: *don't be surprised*. Don't let it catch you off balance, unprepared, not having thought this was involved.

Why do we think that suffering is an unexpected item in the Christian's pilgrimage, when Christ himself suffered and promised no less to anyone who followed him? Read through the teaching of Christ. He made it utterly clear that anybody who really walked with him would suffer sooner or later. We are surprised because we don't know God's Word and man's world well enough. If we knew God's Word better, we would know that God's Word promises suffering in this world and glory in the next. If we knew man's world better, we would know that it is not a world that a Christian can go along with. It is not a world that a Christian can ever feel at home in. It is a world that belongs not to God but to Satan. Indeed, if you want to know what the world is really like, consider this text: "we know that we are of God, but the whole world lies in the power, in the grip of the evil one."

Sooner or later good and evil clash and suffering results for the good, so don't be surprised. It is to be expected. If I have not suffered as a Christian, I am an abnormal Christian. I may be the average Christian in this country but I am not the norm. A normal Christian is one who knows what the cross is, one who knows that before there can be a crown there must be a cross, and one who may even bear in his own body the marks of the Lord Jesus.

When I have met Christians who have suffered for their faith, I have felt they were so much nearer normal than I was – so much nearer Jesus Christ. It is not only usual for Christians to suffer, it is useful for them to suffer. Suffering according to Peter proves you. In other words, it shows you up. It tests. Isn't it wonderful to discover that you really can come through praising God? A little motto on my desk says, "Hallelujah anyway" – it fits every conceivable crisis, circumstance or situation.

If you can go through suffering and say, "Hallelujah anyway," you have proved something. You proved that you loved God for his own sake and not because he gave you a comfortable life. This is what Job was proving in the Old Testament. He nearly fell from time to time, but ultimately he came through and said, "God, you are God and I still praise you." He had come through and he proved for ever that at least there was one man in the human race who loved God for his own sake and could suffer and still say, "Hallelujah." So it is useful to a Christian to suffer because it proves you, and the word "prove" does not just mean "show up" it means to strengthen; it means to test to the point of breaking and find that the strength is there, and that is the great blessing that comes to those who suffered. They have found that the strength was there.

The second thing Peter says is: *Don't be miserable*. So don't be surprised and don't be miserable – but rejoice. That is most unusual. One of the most moving stories I have ever read was the life of Paul Schneider, the pastor in Germany who dared to voice his opinion of Hitler during the 1930s and about what he believed to be a crime against humanity and against God. His congregation begged him not to preach like this. They did not want to lose their pastor; the mayor of the town came and begged him to be silent. They didn't want to lose one of their best citizens, but he went on.

The day came when the Gestapo came and took him away in their lorry, and he said goodbye to his wife and four children and unborn child; he went away in that lorry smiling. I have a book which includes some of his letters, written from the concentration camp where he was starved to death. The word that occurs so frequently in those letters is "joy". When a man does that, he has discovered a secret. Don't be miserable but rejoice. Why should you rejoice? What is there to be happy about when everything seems to fall on you? What is there to be happy about when you are going through suffering?

Thirdly, Peter teaches this: *don't be ashamed*. What a future is laid up for you if you suffer for the Lord Jesus. The cross will give way to the crown. You share Christ's sufferings, you will share the glory that follows them. Go through it with him here, you will reign hereafter. Some of our dear brethren who have really suffered for the Lord are going to be miles above us in heaven. They will be there on thrones with Christ, and with crowns – special crowns for the martyrs. So you can rejoice in your future even if the present is a bit tough. But you can even rejoice in the present. You are blessed; you are to be congratulated. Jesus congratulated those who suffered. Why? Because somehow to suffer for the Lord Jesus brings you close to him. Three men were cast into a fiery furnace because they refused to accept a totalitarian government. Nebuchadnezzar looked into the furnace and said, "There's somebody else with them, somebody else walking in that fire, and the fourth one is like the son of the gods." To go through the fire is to go through it with someone else. Rejoice! No wonder in the New Testament it says that the early apostles rejoiced that they were worthy to suffer for his name. To be envied because you suffer – so, second, don't be miserable when it comes.

Third: *don't be ashamed* though there may be humiliation, indignity involved. Indeed, one has read so many stories in which Christians have been publicly humiliated to try to break their self-respect. Thank God that when you are a real Christian you have no self-respect left to break. The worst that people can say about you isn't bad enough for your real state, but when you are a Christian you can afford to be humiliated because you were that low when you came to Christ – you are a nobody. Don't be ashamed. What would make you ashamed if you have suffered?

Well, I will tell you one thing that would: that you deserved it; that you were partly responsible for it; that you did something to cause it. So Peter is saying be quite sure that they cannot pin anything onto you that would make you so ashamed, because in a day when Christians are being persecuted they must be terribly careful to be upright. Otherwise, if they are persecuted for some wrong in themselves, that is so embarrassing; that would really shame you. "So," says Peter – and it is remarkable to say this to church members – "Don't murder; don't be a thief." But there are two more things that might come more home to us: "Don't be a wrongdoer or a mischief-maker." That implies someone who has deliberately provoked the persecution, someone who has gone out of their way to be awkward; somebody who has got a martyr complex and is determined to be persecuted.

Funnily enough, in the days when Christians were being thrown to the lions in the Roman colosseum, the Christians who weren't caught were so envious of those who were that they deliberately went out of their way to provoke the public authorities – that they might be martyred. That did happen and it was quite a problem in the early church. It could be a problem again if suffering comes. We are never to provoke it; we are not to cause it. I think that raises questions about some forms of public protest if they are deliberately provocative and are deliberately causing offence. We are not to be ashamed of being caught doing things that are wrong, but do not be a wrongdoer, nor a mischief-maker, otherwise you would be ashamed. We are to suffer not as a criminal but as a Christian. There must be nothing pinned on us except that we follow Jesus, no excuse for publicly humiliating us except that we have done what he told us to do and no more.

The fourth thing that Peter teaches us here is that when suffering comes *don't be resentful*. It is difficult to understand suffering in the perspective of this life only. Why should God allow this? I was talking at a school and one of the first questions brought up by the pupils was this: if the Jews are God's chosen people, why did he let six million of them be murdered? As if somehow believing in God should be an insurance policy against all trouble and tragedy. Actually the answer to that question was, "That happened because they were God's people" – not in spite of it but because of it. God had told them it would happen and if you read Deuteronomy 28, it is explained. But let's get back to Peter, who says you must not be resentful. There are times when you say, "Why should I suffer more than other people?"

Bear in mind that first of all judgment begins in the household of God. It is God's way of chastising his people and purifying them and getting them ready. How many members of a congregation would there be if the police were waiting for you outside and you knew it? Would you be in church if you knew that you might be taken away from your family and never see them again because you worshipped with others? God has a way of using suffering to refine his church, to make the believer what he wants that believer to be. Therefore, we should not resent it because God is beginning to deal with the household of God. What we should do is what the Psalmist did: look at the real future of those who do not suffer in this world but are heading for more suffering than we will have in the next.

In a sense, I do believe in purgatory – though not as purgatory after death but as purgatory before death. The fires through which God allows Christians to go do refine them, to make saints of them, and that is purgatory. It means a pruning that they may bring forth more fruit. But compare the believer with the unbeliever. One day the psalmist went to the temple—Psalm 73 is all about it. He went in and he saw God and said, "Oh God, here I am. I've been trying to live right, I've been trying to cleanse my heart and I just go through it. I have one trouble after the other, pain all the day long, and I look at these wicked people and they don't like me any more and they're prosperous and they'll die in peace in bed and they don't have any troubles." He was resentful of the fact that as a believer in God he suffered more than the unbeliever. That can happen.

God told him to look a bit further. Then the Psalmist said, "I perceived their end; they're on a slippery slope and they are going to slide on it and slip off. Their end is destruction whereas you will receive me afterward into glory." He saw the thing in true perspective: the believer suffers in this world; the unbeliever suffers in the next. Which do you really want to be? Don't be resentful if you suffer as a believer more than the unbeliever next door.

Fifthly, *don't be discouraged.* I suppose that this is one of the biggest difficulties a Christian has to fight. I will confess freely to you that one of my biggest besetting temptations is discouragement, to be discouraged in the Lord's work. When things don't go right, when things don't go as you would hope they would go, to be discouraged.

That is why one of the greatest ministries mentioned in the New Testament church is the ministry of encouragement. Barnabas was a man like that – a son of encouragement. What a lovely ministry. You could exercise a great ministry in your church if you did nothing else but encourage other people. To discourage a person is a very naughty thing to do. Suffering can discourage you. You might be tempted to say, "Oh I give up. I've taken just about as much as I can stand."

Richard Wurmbrand was in a cell with another Christian who was being tortured every day. Finally, this other Christian came back to the cell one night after being tortured and said to Richard, "I can't go on. I've had all I can take and tomorrow I will deny Christ." Physical pain had caused him to be discouraged – literally, no more courage left.

That night Richard Wurmbrand tells how he was so desperate for this man's integrity that he crept over to his bunk and put his hands on his throat and was about to strangle him to get him to glory without denying Christ. The man's eyes opened and he said, "What are you doing?" He said, "I was going to kill you to stop you denying Christ." That gave the man courage. The next day he was tortured again and the next day and the next day and the next day for ten more days until he died, but he didn't deny Christ. He wasn't discouraged. He went right on because of that other Christian's determination to see him through.

Don't be discouraged. Why not? Well because you would be ashamed when you met Christ if you were. There are two things to hang on to when you are going through it. I know some people do go through it. You may go through it in your home or at work. It may not be to the point of death by torture, but you do go through it. There are two things to hang on to: *hang on to goodness*; keep your integrity, don't let your principles go under all the pressure that is on you. Never say, "What's the point of being good?" Hang on to your goodness, and the other thing is: *hang on to God*. There is only one place in the New Testament where God is called the Creator and it is here. Hang on to the Creator – the God who made the stars is there, hang on to him.

The suffering that most of us have is the same sort of suffering that other people go through who are not believers, but we are thinking here about the suffering of Christians in particular. Why do they suffer in so many countries in the world? Why do many passages on suffering in the Bible seem irrelevant to us? I came to the conclusion that there are two reasons. I realised that this is not very easy to understand or to accept, but the two reasons I came to were these: first in England our world is too "Christian". Let me hasten to explain what I mean. Christianity has become part of the establishment. Many of the people in this land are christened as babies in a Christian church. Many of them will come to church to be married. Most will be given Christian burials. But I reckon the number of real Christians in this country is somewhere between one and two percent. It is part of the establishment. It has become the accepted order of things. In schools, every day has traditionally begun with prayers and there are R.E. lessons. There are prayers in public institutions, in our law courts, and there are chaplains for this, that, and the other. There are national holidays for Christian festivals. There is a whole block of bishops in the House of Lords. Do you think this is a good or bad thing? I have the feeling that it could be a disaster. It could mean that British people are getting just enough Christianity to inoculate them against the real thing; just enough of a smattering of it to feel that somehow they are Christians. One of the commonest things I get told and I get tired of people saying this is: "I think you can be a Christian without going to church" – as if the logical deduction from that is that if you don't go to church, you are much more likely to be a Christian.

So we have this vague, generalised, "Christian England" in which people think they are Christians already. Therefore they are neither for nor against Christ. They can afford to be indifferent to us as long as we will go on "hatching, matching, and dispatching" them. We have got into a world that is too "Christian" to be converted, which has a smattering of it all but does not know the reality or the power of godliness. That is one factor. I came to the conclusion that if Buddhism or, even more, Islam were the established religion in this land then we would know suffering very quickly. The second reason is this, and I found this even harder to face: I believe that we do not experience as much suffering in this country because our Christianity is too worldly. There isn't a difference or a contrast between us. When the world gets "Christian" and the Christian gets too worldly there won't be suffering; there won't be persecution.

These two reasons I have given you are seen most clearly at Christmas time. Both tendencies are there which is why Christmas can come and go without people getting converted. I have read that in fact there is a slump in conversions around Christmas. This is in spite of the fact that there are carols being sung everywhere; in spite of the fact that there are nativity plays, and shop windows displaying a babe in a manger, there is a slump in evangelism at that time. Why? What has happened? The world has got too "Christian" at Christmas and got just enough of the Christmas story to be inoculated against the real, hard facts of Christmas – that when Jesus was born, hundreds of innocent babies were slaughtered (when did you last see that on a Christmas card?); and that when Jesus came into the world an old man prophesied that this child would be set for the rise and fall of many. It is not true to say that man shall live for evermore because of Christmas day. Some will, but some will die eternally. So the world has just enough Christianity in it around Christmas time and is willing to sing carols – but not too much preaching, please.

I was invited to preach at a carol service some time ago and I did preach – but now they have gone back to just having carols. I maybe said too much! So far and no further. Let me ask, do Christians not get a bit too worldly at Christmas? Will your celebration of Christmas be no different from the next-door neighbour other than the fact that you went to church? Or do we get so caught up in this commercialised jamboree that we will overeat and we will over-drink and simply live it up? You may already be up to your neck with family bills. Has the Christmas tradition of giving unneeded and often unwanted gifts become an unbearable burden?

Has the obligation of gift buying cut into your savings until giving for gospel work had to be sliced thin or suspended for the season?

The very essence of Christmas is evangelism because Christ Jesus came into the world to save sinners. Yet it is a fact that in most churches Christmas is the least evangelistic season of the year. In spite of all our activities, December is the weakest month of the year from the standpoint of winning souls. Personal work almost comes to a halt. Missionary giving declines shamefully. Evangelistic events are practically eliminated. Time is consumed with holiday preparations and money is used for gifts, which are soon set aside and forgotten. A writer said, "I have been in Tokyo in Japan during Christmas. Santa Clauses, reindeer, and gaudy Christmas trees literally cluttered the city. Stores bulged with colourful wares, human traffic making them like madhouses. The most commercialised Christmas stampede we had ever seen and yet this was in a land where the Christ of Christmas was practically unknown." Does that make you feel uncomfortable? Is our ineffectiveness and lack of suffering due to the fact that we have got caught up in it too, and we enjoy it all too much even to ask radical questions?

What would happen if Christians said, "This is not the way to celebrate the coming of the Saviour"? This mad jamboree of spending is just not the way to worship Jesus? Supposing we all said that and supposing we all acted on it – you would soon have the chamber of commerce making comments. You would begin to find that when the world and Christians behave differently, suffering begins to come and so I want to leave you with that uncomfortable thought.

Is it because our world is too "Christian" and our Christianity is too worldly that these lessons on suffering which were put in the Bible to help us are not relevant? To our brethren and sisters in other parts of the world they are.

What I am saying is this: Christians are no longer a threat to society and Christians are no longer a threat to Satan. Therefore the world can afford to ignore or patronise us.

It is when the people of God live practical holiness and pursue effective evangelism that they will be called upon to suffer in the name of Jesus. When we do, let us rejoice that we are worthy to do so.

9

CONCLUSION

Read 1 Peter 5:1–14

A. ELDERS (1–4)

    1. Caring shepherds (1–3)
      a. Not reluctant but eager
      b. Not greedy but serving
      c. Not bossy but exemplary
    2. Chief Shepherd (4)
      a. Crown of glory
      b. Never fading

B. YOUNGERS (5–11)

    1. Human responsibility (5–9)
      a. Humble
          i. To older; ii. To one another
      b. Heedful
          i. Controlling self; ii. Resisting Satan
    2. Divine response (10–11)
      a. Restore after suffering
      b. Strengthen until steadfast

FINAL GREETINGS (12–14)

    1. FROM US (12–13)
      a. Brother Silas
      b. Son Mark
    2. TO YOU (14)
      a. Kiss for each
      b. Peace to all

1 Peter 5 is a "love song" for those who love the Lord. You know that life does not consist of possessions but of people. Life does not consist of achievements but of attitudes. Life does not consist of reputation but of relationships. That is why at the end of his letter Peter draws together a number of threads about attitudes and relationships. There are four of them in this chapter: your attitude to the church and relationships within it; your attitude to God; your attitude to the devil, and your attitude to suffering.

These four simple notes that are struck make up a lovely chord of Christian living. First of all, then, your *attitudes and relationships within the church*. When you are born again you are born again into a family. You not only have a new Father, you have got new brothers and sisters and you have older brothers and sisters too. Relationships within the family of God are like relationships in any family. In particular, younger and older need to get on together. Therefore, Peter talks first of all to those whom he describes as elders and then he talks to those who are younger. He talks about their attitudes to each other. The one place the generation gap must never appear is in the church of Jesus Christ. I have heard it said that the only gap in the church is the regeneration gap: between those who have been born again and those who haven't. But those who have been born again know no differences of age, sex, class, or anything else in their attitudes to one another.

Let us look at what Peter says to the elders. The word "elder" is very interesting. Originally it was a physical word

meaning anybody over forty, but it means much more than
that here. In the Bible the word "elder" became a spiritual
word, meaning someone who has matured more than others
in the Christian life, who has travelled either more quickly
or further than others. It is interesting that you could be a
spiritual elder within twelve months of your conversion if
you were spiritually more mature than others converted at
the same time.

When Paul started a church he would go back to it a year
later and would appoint elders, those who had made most
progress, who were maturing and were leading the others.
But it is more than that – it is a plural noun not an adjective
so it doesn't refer to everybody who is maturing. It refers
to those who have been set apart by the church to be elders,
those who are recognised as being spiritual leaders and who
are appointed to this office.

Peter humbly describes himself as a "fellow elder". He
could have said, "I was the chief apostle." He could have
said, "I was the first appointed leader of the Gentile Christian
church," but he didn't. He said, "I'm your fellow elder. I'm
just like you, someone who was chosen for this office to
look after the sheep." If you belong to a family when you
are a Christian, you will also belong to a flock. Peter was
told by Jesus, "Feed my lambs, look after them." That is an
elder's job.

The elders are told three things about the motives of an
elder: the inner workings of his heart while he's doing his
job. First, he must do it not because he must but because
he may – not out of a sense of duty but out of a sense of
privilege and honour. It is something he should gladly accept
as an office in the church. Not because the church has voted
him in and therefore he has got to do it, but he would love
to do it – not because he is being coerced or pressed into it.

Secondly, he must do it not to get but to give. Of course,

any office among any group of people enables you to get things for yourself. Any possession of leadership or responsibility can produce selfish motives of gain. But Peter is saying: not for what you can get out of it but for what you can put into it.

Thirdly he says it is not to lord it over people but to lead them; not to domineer but to guide. A shepherd looking after the flock isn't a dictator but he is a leader. A shepherd in the Middle East doesn't chase up the sheep from behind—that is how we do it in this country, but when our Lord talked about the shepherd he was thinking of sheep in the Middle East, where the shepherd leads. This is the way you ought to walk in. This is where the right pasture lies. Shepherds are to be examples to them. Here is the pattern for an elder: you walk in the right way and they can follow.

Why should an elder behave like this? Because – and here is an interesting thing – Peter says, "You have an archbishop and his name is Jesus." The title given to Jesus here in this verse is "archbishop". The word "bishop" means no more than a shepherd. That is why those who today call themselves "bishop" usually carry a shepherd's crook. All those who have been called to be elders in the flock are bishops, shepherds. They are to be shepherds, bishops, because there is (and the singular word we can render "archbishop" is used here) only one archbishop – Jesus. He is the great shepherd, the good shepherd. Elders are under-shepherds and one day he will reward those who are faithful in looking after the flock. That is the motive. The only thing you are allowed to look at as an elder – something that you will get – is the wreath that Jesus places on the brow of a good shepherd. You may look forward to that.

He doesn't say "Now you youngers" – because to be younger is not an office in the church. He means those who are not elders. You who are growing in the faith, you who have just started the Christian life, what about you? Here comes something rather unpopular. There are two sides to a flock. There is the shepherd one side and the sheep the other. The relationship has got to be right both ways. Do you remember the song of Deborah in the Old Testament, after the battle against Sisera? She praised the Lord for two things: that the leaders led and that the people followed. Blessed be the name of the Lord. Those are two great blessings in a flock when shepherds lead properly and sheep follow properly – then you have got a happy relationship.

Now what kind of following? Peter says quite bluntly, "You that are younger be subject...." He has already told citizens to be subject to rulers. He has already told wives to be subject to husbands. He has already told employees to be subject to employers. He now says, "Sheep, be subject to shepherds." Why does he say that? Because when you are young you tend to be headstrong, critical, arrogant, and self-willed. Does that sound a bit strong? But I have been young and I know that when you are young, you think you can put the world right. A younger Christian in the first flash of knowing Jesus may look at older Christians and say, "Why aren't they more enthusiastic?"

But "be subject to the elders" means: recognise that some of those quieter people sitting around you have walked through many experiences with Christ. They have been through deep times, they have had battles that you know nothing about yet. They have been around more corners than you have and they could teach you a thing or two if you gave them a chance – the youngers and the elders fitting together. One thing that pleased me most, I think, as a Pastor was to see that happen and to see younger people and older people talking together, praying together, loving together, witnessing together. That is how it should be and I pray it will always continue – the younger and the older helping one another. I believe you can learn from each other. I believe older ones need to recapture something of the thrill and the wonder and the first love of a young person who has just come to Jesus. I believe you younger ones need to know something of the stability, perseverance and loyalty of older ones – the family of God learning to live together. Why should younger ones pay attention to older ones? Because God resists the proud, God doesn't like people who think they know everything. God doesn't like people who can teach everybody else but themselves, he cuts them down to size.

That brings us to the second relationship mentioned here: *our attitude to God*. When we are accepted through Christ, God is our Father, and he does two things which every good father does. Number one, he disciplines; number two he cares. It is because of the Father's discipline and care that you can trust him.

Therefore we are told two things. First: be humbled toward God and he will exalt you – if you want to be great, and doesn't every Christian want to be a great saint? Of course we do. There is a Christian ambition, you want to be a great worker for the Lord. If you don't feel that, then have you seen him properly? You are bound to want to be a great Christian but remember that it is those who humble themselves who become great. He will exalt. He is a God who will discipline you. Indeed the letter to the Hebrews says this: "If you are not chastised of the Lord then you are a bastard." That is a strong statement. But if you never feel the hand of God disciplining you, spanking you spiritually, then you can't be a true child of his because whom the Lord loves he chastens. Humble yourselves therefore before Almighty God and in due season he will exalt you – lift you up again. The second thing we need before God is serenity. Cast your cares on him for he cares about you. One of the things that one envies children having is that carefree attitude to life. Watch little children playing – how carefree they can be. I remember how carefree I was as a child. I would run out and play in the street with all my friends up the road and come in at one o'clock and expect lunch to be on the table, and it always was because somebody cared – so my life was carefree because someone cared. That is a true parent and God is a true Father and we can live a carefree life.

There are two ways of being carefree. One is to be careless, giving no thought to a problem, and that kind of carefree attitude is dangerous and wrong. But there is another carefree attitude: He cares about me; "I've taken this thing that was worrying me stiff, I've taken this burden and this problem and I've given it to him and he's going to sort it out." That's why Jesus taught that worry is a sin – because if you are worried then it is virtually atheism. You are saying: I have no father to look after me. I've got to sort it out all by myself. I'm an orphan alone in the world. Instead, cast all your care on him for he cares about you.

The third attitude we need to get right to go into the future is our *attitude to Satan*. I wonder if anybody has really discovered God without discovering Satan. You may not discover Satan straightaway but very soon after your Christian life has begun you say, "Why is it such a battle? Why is it that I just can't get through? Why is it that I'm having all these problems and temptations? Who is getting at me, trying to stop me going forward?" The answer is, "When you got converted you turned one of your best friends into one of your worst enemies." Satan himself didn't like you one bit. How do you deal with him? Well first of all, you must be alert; you must never forget him. That is why Jesus, when he taught a daily prayer, included in that prayer a reference to the devil. He said: When you pray, say, "Give us today our daily bread and lead us not into temptation but deliver us from the evil one." What a pity the Lord's Prayer got changed. Never forget the devil, he is around the whole time. It is when you have forgotten that he is there that he pounces.

I will never forget one fascinating railway journey that my wife and I made in the heart of Africa. It was the single, old narrow gauge railway line from Mombasa to Nairobi. I remembered, as we wound our way up to the plateau of Nairobi in that old train, the story of the building of that railway. The greatest hazard they faced was lions. They lost so many men with lions that finally they had to divide the men into two groups and one group watched for lions and the other laid the sleepers and put the steel rails on them, because the lion doesn't give you any warning. Before they had the guards out the lions would just prowl through the bush and pounce. The devil, says Peter, is like a prowling lion. You don't make jokes about prowling lions. You don't treat them lightly. We must remember every day that the devil doesn't like us. How do you deal with him? The answer is by standing firm. I am told, though I have never had the opportunity or the willingness to put it to the test, that if a lion comes at you, stand still. I hope you remember that advice and have the presence of mind to do it. There are cases known of this. I believe David Livingstone had this once (though he had an unfortunate occasion as well with another lion that mauled him) –stand still, don't shift, and resist. Peter uses the word "firm" – stand firm. Don't show fear. You are not afraid of the devil because there is somebody standing right with you who is stronger than he is. Stand firm, resist the devil and it is he who will turn away and run. So here is our attitude to the devil: be alert and be firm. Like every bully, he is bluffing. A Christian can call his bluff and say, "You're a bully and you're a coward and in the name of Christ, go." He hates me for telling you this.

Which brings us to the fourth thing. This is now the fifth time Peter has mentioned suffering – once in each chapter. When *suffering* comes, God may let you go through it for a little while. God has never promised to give Christians an easy, comfortable life – he has promised to let you go through it for a while. When you go through it next and when you face a tough passage and when someone you thought was your friend turns out to be the opposite, and when people laugh at you for being interested in the things of Christ, when you feel alone, here are two things: first, be patient because all Christians suffer. You are not going through anything new. There are Christians all over the world going through suffering and many of them far worse suffering than you are experiencing. Your brotherhood is a brotherhood of suffering; it is a family of suffering that you have been born into. Second, be confident because God will see you through.

After a little while, God will do four things and they are lovely words. He will *restore,* and the word Peter uses is a word for mending nets or for mending fractured bones. Isn't that a lovely word? When you are feeling that your net is broken and that your bones are broken, God will mend. Second, God will *establish*, which means to make you solid. Suffering is usually one of God's ways of making you a solid Christian. You may be a lively one before you have suffered but you will be a solid one after you have suffered. Thirdly, he will *strengthen* you. You come out of suffering not a weaker person but a stronger one. Fourthly, he will *settle* you. The word means to lay a foundation and Peter was thinking back to the days when he was named "Simon", which means a reed – easily blown about. Jesus called him "Peter", a rock, because the Lord was going to make him a foundation – and he did, and he achieved it.

In the closing part of the letter Peter includes a few little personal comments. A message from Silvanus, a secretary he shared with Paul. Silvanus must have taken down some letters in his time. He sends greetings from what he calls "Babylon", which is the early Christian nickname for Rome. He sends personal greetings and asks them to be sure to give each other love.

Remember he was writing in the days of Nero and he himself was going to die in the arena in just a few months' time. He knows that a storm of persecution is breaking in the capital city of the empire and will reach the furthermost shores. He is writing to Asia Minor to prepare them, and his last word is "peace" – to those who are in Christ. There is no peace to anybody else, but to those who are in Christ there is.

Sadhu Sundar Singh, was a great Indian Christian. After he became a Christian he was turned out of his family. They even held a funeral service over him and he went away. He was bitterly persecuted and one day his enemies got hold of him, tied him to a stake and put leeches all over his body to suck his blood until he died. For three days he went through that, but he survived. They cut him down after three days. The leader of the gang that had tied him there said, "How could you have such peace during these three days?" The Sadhu told them about the peace Jesus gives – not the kind of peace that depends on nice circumstances or everything going smoothly. Peace be to them that are in Christ – if the storm comes; if the persecution comes; if the suffering comes. Now two key words seem to shine out for Peter: *grace* and *glory*. One is the beginning of the Christian life; the other is the end of it – from grace to glory. You began by grace; you finish in glory. Peter, beginning with the grace of Christ in chapter 1, lands us in glory in chapter 5.

10

EDUCATION

Read 2 Peter 1:1–15

Introduction (1–2)

        Two names (Simon Peter); Two letters (I, II Peter)

        Two titles (servant, apostle); Two persons (God, Jesus)

        Two greetings (grace, peace)

A. MATHEMATICS (3–4)

        1. Equation

                a. Sin – down to same level

                b. Salvation – up to same level

        2. Multiplication

                a. Grace

                b. Peace

        3. Addition

                a. Life – his glory

                b. Godliness – his excellence

        4. Subtraction

                a. Passions

                b. Partakers

B. MATRICULATION (5–15)

    1. UP A LADDER (5–11)

        a. Rungs (5–7)

          i. Faith; ii. Virtue; iii. Knowledge; iv. Self-control;

          v. Steadfastness; vi. Godliness; vi. Brotherly affection;

          viii. Love.

        b. Top (8)

          i. Effective; ii. Fruitful

        c. Bottom (9)

          i. Short-sighted; ii. Forgetful

        d. Up (10a); e. Down (10b); f. Above (11)

    2. UNDER A LEADER (12–15)

        Remind while alive (12–13)

        Remember when dead (14–15)

Peter's two letters deal with two quite different aspects of the Christian life. The first dealt with the enemies of Christ outside the church; the second with the enemies of Christ inside. The latter are the more difficult, the more dangerous. He deals in this letter with false teachers, for example, those who actually teach inside the church – but teach wrong things. He deals with the battles we have inside us with our own passions and wrong desires.

If the key word in the first letter was "suffering", the key word (occurring sixteen times in the second, shorter one), is "knowledge." Here, Peter is concerned that you may grow in grace and in the knowledge of our Lord Jesus Christ. So we get a change of emphasis between the two letters. Not only has he written two letters but he usually gives himself two names – this is a letter from *Simon Peter* and we have already noted the significance of those two names.

He also describes himself in two titles: "servant" and "apostle" or, quite literally, "slave" and "apostle". The interesting thing is that "slave" is a low word, from the bottom of the social ladder, and "apostle" is a very high word, meaning an envoy, an ambassador. It seems as if Peter has a really good view of himself. He sees himself as right at the bottom, yet in Christ he sees himself lifted up to serve as an apostle. You can't be either a slave or an apostle without someone else. No one can make themselves a slave. No one can make themselves an apostle. A slave has to be bought by someone else; an apostle has to be sent by someone else. So what Peter is telling us is: What I am, I am because someone else made me; somebody else bought me, which makes me a slave; somebody else sent me, which makes me an apostle. The "someone else" is undoubtedly the Lord Jesus Christ.

I could put the rest of the first four verses in the form of a Christian mathematics lesson! It is knowledge that we need if we are to grow. 1 Peter was concerned with being born and he began by saying, "We've been born anew." But 2 Peter begins by telling us how to grow. It is not enough just to be converted and be born again, we want to grow, and grow up.

Now here are the five signs of Christian mathematics, which you need to know to help you to grow up. The first is the *equal* sign. Peter addresses those who have obtained a faith of "equal standing with ours in the righteousness of our God and Saviour, Jesus Christ". One of the first things to learn in the Christian life is that you are equal with everybody else who shares faith. Faith is the great leveller of the Christian life. We tend to divide people up into grades and classes and groups. We have got our own classification of our fellow men and women. But God has only one: you are all sinners and you are all saved by faith. He brings you right down to the equality of sin and shows you that it doesn't matter whether you are good or bad, rich or poor, wise or simple – you have fallen short of God's glory.

I remember somebody bringing that home very vividly by describing graphically three men standing on a rock, fishing at the edge of the sea and not noticing that the tide had come in and surrounded the rock. When they noticed it was too late, and there was already between them and the mainland a gulf filled with water. So the first one tried to jump, and he made it about halfway across and fell in. The second one after some hesitation went back a bit, took a flying leap, and he made it three quarters of the way and fell in. The third one, who was an athlete, went right back tensed his muscles, took a marvellous leap, and he only failed by six inches. But they all fell short, and they all fell in. The Bible is saying quite simply we have all fallen short of the glory of God. You can say, "Well I've only fallen short by six inches." Do you think that makes you any safer than somebody who fell short by a mile? Do you think that because you are not a criminal or a cannibal, somehow that improves you in the sight of God? We are all equal in this: we all fell short. It doesn't matter by how much, we fell short. That bit between the falling short and God's ideal needs forgiveness and faith.

I will never forget one experience in which this came home to me. I was in the city of Rome one Easter. On Easter Sunday morning I was down in a cellar at a communion service. I suppose we were about five hundred yards from the Vatican, and we could hear the crowds up in the street shouting. But we gathered in this cellar, packed with people just to take bread and wine on Easter Sunday morning. I remember as I came to take the wine and bread I saw kneeling in front of me a very wealthy man. He looked and breathed money, you could tell. Next to him was a beggar from the streets of Rome in rags – the very rich and the very poor. To see them kneel together and to take one cup and pass it from one to the other, to take one loaf and pass it – I just saw the equal sign in God's mathematics. People would look at the outside of those two. God would say: "You are both sinners; you both have faith in my Son. You have an equal standing before me." That means that there are no distinctions among us and we make no classification of each other. We are all one in Christ Jesus. We make no distinctions. When we take that one loaf and share it together it symbolises that we are one Body in Christ.

I think of a communion service in the Forces, in the Middle East. As the soldiers got up to go forward to receive the bread and wine, a private noticed that he was stepping out in front of his major and he immediately, instinctively, stepped back.

But the major stepped back and said, "Everywhere else, but not here." The equal sign! It is great to get out of the rat race and to lose all desire for status symbols. It is great to get rid of both your superiority complexes and your inferiority complexes and learn the equal sign to all those who have an equal standing of faith in our God and Saviour Jesus Christ.

The next sign you need to learn in God's mathematics is the *multiply* sign, "Grace and peace be multiplied to you in the knowledge of God and of Jesus our Lord." Do you think you have found all the grace and peace that God has for you? You have only just begun to find it! To multiply means to increase rapidly. It occurs right at the beginning of the Bible, "Go into the earth and multiply," says God to man and the animals. Multiply, increase rapidly – may grace and peace be multiplied to you. One of those is the root, the other is the fruit. When you have the root of grace then you will have the fruit of peace. You can have neither without the other. You cannot have the grace of God without the peace of God resulting. You cannot have the peace of God until you have found the grace of God. You found both when you became a Christian. But do you think you've found it all? Oh no, you have only just begun to find a bit of it. God can multiply his grace and peace. How does he do it? By the knowledge of Jesus. That is why teaching has always been a ministry in the church. But there is a danger that we learn *about* Jesus without learning Jesus.

I remember being told about two little boys coming out of a Sunday school in Tynemouth, Northumberland. One boy said to the other, "Do you know Jesus?" He said, "Well, I should do. I've been coming to this Sunday school for years. They're always on about him." The first boy said, "No, I didn't mean that. I meant do you know him to talk to?" The knowledge that helps us to grow is the knowledge of a person. How do you get to know a person? There are two simple ways. One is to talk with them. You notice I don't say to talk *to* them. If you just talk to someone they will get to know you, but you don't get to know them. But to talk to Jesus and listen as well, you get to know him. The second way you get to know people is by living with them so that you go through crises together, so that you really see how they react and how they behave in a crisis. That is why you can go to church regularly and see someone and recognise their face and say hello without ever really getting to know them, because you don't live with them. You don't see that church member on Monday morning. You don't see them when everything has gone wrong. You don't see them when they are suddenly facing a crisis. If you did see them then you would know them. As you live with Jesus not just on Sunday, but Monday to Saturday, and go through crises with him and find out how he really reacts, you get to know him. As you do, grace and peace are multiplied. You thought that your conversion was wonderful, you thought the early months of your Christian life was great, but the thing is just multiplying. It gets greater and greater.

I wonder how often you have had this experience. I have gone away from a service and said, "Lord, that's the climax. We'll never have a better service than that. We'll never feel your presence more real than that." Lo and behold, next Sunday it has been better still. The Christian life is like that. You think you have had a good year and if you really get to know Jesus better, if you talk with him, live with him – not just on Sundays, but every day – you will find that grace and peace multiply. It is the second sign of Christian mathematics.

The third sign is the *plus*. I know the word is not in the passage and I am not even sure that Peter would know it. What do I mean by it? It says here that God has added to your life everything you need for life and godliness. Let me start in a simple way. I used to like making models when I was a boy. I am afraid I have not grown out of that. But model kits have changed since those days. The ones I used to get you bought, having saved up hard for it, and then you proudly took the box home and you opened it up and found that there was no glue in it, no paint, and that it would need a piece of special wire that you would have to go and find somewhere. There were so many things missing that you didn't feel like starting it! Nowadays, when you open up a model kit you find everything you need. All that is left is to get on with it. Peter says that divine power has granted to us all things that pertain to life and godliness. You have a complete "kit" from God. Everything you need to be a saint, everything you need to live the holy life is all there for you.

There is nothing novel about these things, they are the same as were there in those days. He has given you the opportunity of *prayer.* A Christian can pray as nobody else can pray. He has given you a *Bible* to read, and there is no substitute for meditation in God's Word and there never will be – there is no shortcut. He has given you *Christian fellowship.* That is one of the strongest factors in growing up. I don't know what I would have done if there had not been the right kind of fellowship for me to get into after I became a Christian. You will never grow up if you only go to services on Sunday. You need fellowship as well as worship. You need to get into a smaller group where you can pray together, talk together and unburden your heart together, and minister to each other. Fellowship helps you to grow. But above all, God has provided his divine power, the power of the Holy Spirit. Many Christians have not even begun to be aware of the ways God the Holy Spirit teaches, and helps you to grow and helps you to witness. After Jesus rose from the dead, the disciples were thrilled that he was alive. They were ready to do anything for him, they thought. But he told them to wait until they were endued with power.

The next sign is what I would call the *division* sign. Why does that come in the Christian life? That you may escape from the corruption that is in the world because of passion. Make no mistake about it, part of Christian life is separation. There will be division, and it is a division from a rotten world. One of the things about decay that is most disturbing is that it is contagious. That is why I go to my dentist every six months, because if there is decay and rottenness in one tooth it is going to spread quickly. You store your apples for the winter, and if you put one rotten apple in among them expect trouble. Decay must be dealt with drastically.

Wilfred Grenfell tells an almost blood curdling story of his days in Labrador where a man was cut off from civilisation in some remote hut. He and his daughter lived there through the Labrador winter. One day she got frostbite in her legs and it became gangrenous. Finally the father had to take an axe and chop her legs off, then bring her to the hospital. He saved her life in doing so. He knew that he had to stop that and get rid of it. Now Peter says quite bluntly: "It's a rotten world that you live in." It is a rotten world, and you will need to divide from that rottenness. It doesn't mean you've got to separate from people. But it does mean that you have to separate from the rottenness that there is, and that costs something.

Look at three words here. The first is *passions*. Some people think that the church is against any human desire, any natural appetite. That is not true. Christ was not against natural desire. But where it has become a passion then it has become something dangerous – where a desire has become your master instead of remaining your servant. When pride, greed, lust, sloth or malice has so gripped someone that it has taken him or her over, then beware. Jesus said something that Grenfell would have understood: "If your foot offends you, cut it off, it is going to drag you to hell. If your hand offends you, cut it off, it is going to drag you to hell. If your eye causes you to stumble, pluck it out." Did he mean that we should maim our bodies? No – it is a vivid figure of speech meaning this: if there is anything you look at, anything you handle, or anywhere you go on your two feet that is causing you to get rotten, cut it out; divide from it even at the cost of surgery. So that is the division sign – *passions*.

The next word is *promises*. You can do this because he has promised to help you. Think of his promises. He has promised never to let you be tempted too greatly. He has promised to keep from you any temptation that is too much for you to stand. What a lovely promise. That means there is nothing too much for me. Finally, he says, "... so that you may be *partakers* of the divine nature." My real problem is this: when I was born, my nature was born into a rotten world, and that rottenness was in my nature too. How do you deal with that? By trying to reform yourself, crucify yourself? Yes – but more than that, by allowing the divine nature to replace your human nature, to become partakers of him instead of you.

The last sign to mention is one that is not there at all, but makes the number up to five. However, it is in the other four by implication: the *minus* or subtraction sign. Behind all the first four signs is one very simple sign and it is this: less of self and more of Christ. That is the secret of growing up in the Christian life – to cure self-aggrandisement, to cure self-indulgence, to cure self-consciousness, not by trying to get over them, but by killing self. I remember in Kenya meeting a lovely missionary. An African talked to me about that missionary and said, "I have met many unselfish people, but that person is selfless." What a tribute! Many unselfish people had a struggle to deny themselves, but that person was selfless: no self left to pity, no self left to be sensitive, no self left to hurt, a person who has got rid of self can't be hurt any more, there is no self to hurt. The minus sign in the Christian life is to say, "Less of self, more of you", until you can finally say: "none of self. It has all been subtracted. It has all gone; the old me has been crossed out. And I live, yet no longer I, but Christ lives in me."

Now it is, in a sense, a lesson of gymnastics. There is need for exercise and effort, the need to use spiritual energy to develop spiritual muscles. Indeed, the lessons we have here are concerned with spiritual fitness.

Peter gives us seven steps in growing in the Christian life in the direction of Christian maturity. If you think of this like a ladder, then of course the ladder must stand on faith – that is the foundation. If you don't believe in Jesus you are not going anywhere, you haven't started the Christian life. It does not matter how good you are or how bad you are or how mixed you are, you haven't even got a ladder to climb. So we are taking that for granted.

In every career or calling there is a ladder to climb. One business man cynically told me that in business you climb the ladder by treading on those under you and licking the boots of the person above you. But you don't climb the Christian ladder that way! Look instead at the Christian ladder. There is an ambition in the Christian life, a desire to get on. But let us see what kind of ambition. Here is the first step up the ladder: Peter says, "Add to your faith, *virtue*". The word translated "virtue" here is a Greek word that is better translated, "excellence; excellent". It basically means to get above average, to excel. When I used to look through my children's homework books I sometimes found just the one word "Excellent". It means the person had put a bit more effort in, had really gone at it hard, wanted to make a good job of it. You believe in Christ – then add to your faith excellence. Seek to do a bit better than average, put some effort into it. Make a good job of it. Don't be content to be an average Christian. You want to be an excellent Christian. Elsewhere in the Bible the word "excellence" is applied to Jesus. That gives you your standard for excellent work. An excellent mark will go to those who seek to follow him and who seek to climb that ladder of Christian maturity towards Christlikeness.

The second step up in Christian maturity: add to your excellence, or your virtue, *knowledge*. Never despise knowledge. We are called to love God with all our minds. But it is knowledge of a particular kind. It is not knowledge that you get solely from books though, quite frankly, Christians are not reading as they should. We have as many books as we could wish for, to get knowledge about the Christian life. I hope you are a reader and that you discipline yourself to read the Bible and books that will help you to understand and apply what you read in the Bible. But the kind of knowledge Peter means here is not just head knowledge. It is heart knowledge of a person. You get that by spending time with them, talking with them, sharing your life with them.

The third step up is this: add to your knowledge *self-control*. The word literally means "a grip on yourself". That will not come early in the Christian life when you first believe. It is one of the maturing stages to get a grip on yourself, to be in control of yourself rather than having yourself control you.

The fourth step up the ladder is *steadfastness*. The word means to be able to stand firm under pressure. If self-control is concerned more with our pleasures, endurance or steadfastness is concerned with our sorrows. When you are going through it, can you stand firm? That is a mark of getting well up the ladder of Christian maturity.

The next step up is the step of *godliness*. That is a word which has almost gone out of our vocabulary and we don't use it in ordinary conversation. I think I would retranslate it "reverence". Respect for God, for his people, for his name, for his world, for your brother – "reverence". Springing from a reverence for God – that is what godliness means. Add to that, step number six, *brotherly affection*. The Greek word translated by these two English words is *philadelphia*. It was the dream of those who founded the city of Philadelphia in the United States that it would be the first city on earth to be filled with brotherly affection. I am afraid it is not if you go there today. But they lifted that word straight out of the New Testament. To have brotherly affection – it is a warm word. It is primarily relating to your fellow Christians – your brother. It is interesting that Peter puts it well up the ladder. It is not something that is easy at first. Sometimes one of the most difficult things to learn in your Christian life is how to integrate with other Christians. It is much easier to run away from them sometimes and be a Christian on your own. But God intends you to be part of a family, and brotherly affection is a mark of Christian maturity.

Finally, to cap it all, the top rung of the ladder: you have really arrived at Christian maturity when your life is full of *love*. The Greek word translated "love" here (*agape*), was hardly ever used in the ancient Greek world. It is a word that Christians seized on because it is a rare virtue to find. They said: this is the word we want to use for God's love for us and our love for each other and for our neighbour. It is a word that means to be able to love someone when there is nothing lovable in them to love. All other forms of human love are a response to something in the other person that draws your love out. When two young people fall in love it is because they have seen something in the other person that they are attracted to. The Bible never uses this particular word for that kind of love, though that is a valid and a good kind of love that God created – man for woman. But it is a love that has been attracted by the person who is loved. Even brotherly love is based on the fact that he is my brother.

But the kind of word that is translated as "love" here, and is used everywhere for God's love, is the kind which is so spontaneous that it springs out of me towards anyone – and it does not matter whether they are lovable or not. That is the kind of love that God has for you. It is not that he looked down from heaven and said, "I rather like that person," or, "How attractive they are." He looked down and he saw selfish, proud, impatient people, but he loved them. Why? Because he is love. One of the loveliest things in the Old Testament is in the Book of Deuteronomy. God says to the Jews, "Why do you think I love you?" Quite a question. I'm sure that they could have given a number of answers. But the answer is this: God says, "I love you because I love you." There was no reason in them, the reason is in him. We need to reach the point where we can love people not because we like them, not because they are lovable, but because we love.

There was a dramatic conversation between Simon Peter, the writer of this letter, and Jesus, on the shores of Galilee after Jesus rose from the dead and before he ascended to heaven. I am going to give you a literal translation of what went on between them. Jesus said to Peter, "Simon, son of Jonas, do you love me?"

Peter said, "Lord, I have brotherly affection for you."

Jesus said a second time, "Simon, son of Jonas, do you love me?"

Peter said, "I have brotherly affection for you."

So the third time Jesus said, "Simon, son of Jonas, do you have brotherly affection for me?"

Peter was troubled because the third time Jesus said "brotherly affection". Peter, honest now to the last ditch, said, "Lord, you know everything...." He was not going to profess what he hadn't got or to claim to have got higher up the ladder. He really did have affection. But did he dare yet use the word Jesus used of his love? Here is Peter thirty years later, saying that when you can develop the kind of love that goes far beyond human affection you really are learning to grow up in the Christian life.

A great preacher said over three hundred years ago in one sentence: "Each step gives birth to and facilitates the next; each subsequent quality balances and brings to perfection the one preceding." That is quite a sentence. It was a man who had a great influence on John Wesley, incidentally.

It is not easy to climb. Peter uses words like "effort", "zeal", "determination". There is a place for resting in Christ; there is a place for effort for him – and the New Testament balances both. Never drop the one or the other. Never think that the Christian life is all resting and never think it is all effort. It is both. The Good Shepherd knows that sheep need both. He makes us lie down in green pastures and rest, and he leads us beside the still waters, and he makes us walk along the path of righteousness. He gets us going, makes us rest. The Christian life is a combination of resting and effort. Peter is here concerned with the effort.

What happens when you get to the top of the ladder? Peter says you will be effective and fruitful. If these things don't happen to you, if you are just at the bottom of the ladder, if you believe – if you have got faith but if you haven't started to climb, you are not going to be effective or fruitful. You won't have helped anybody else by your life. If you will set as your goal the top of this ladder you will become increasingly effective as a Christian. You don't want to be a useless Christian. You don't want to be a passenger in the gospel train. There is no room for passengers, God wants crew. He wants you to be useful and effective in your own way, and you need to be on the way up this ladder to be increasingly useful and effective.

What happens if you stay at the bottom of the ladder? Peter says you are short-sighted and forgetful. Short-sighted? What does he mean? Well, because you can't see the top of the ladder you can't see anything more. You say, "I'm a believer, I'm alright, I'm going to heaven. There's nothing more to it." You are short-sighted – you can't see any further than your conversion. If you were called upon to give a testimony and to talk about the Lord Jesus it shouldn't stop at your conversion, it should start there. Then you go on to say what he has done for you since. But some people, if they were asked to give their testimony, would tell you how they were converted and then stop – short-sighted. God wants you to have a vision of the goal ahead, like Paul saying, "I forget the things that are behind, and I stretch forward, I strain at it, towards the future, the things that lie ahead, the prize of the high calling of God in Christ Jesus."

Peter not only says you are short-sighted, he says that you have forgotten something – you have forgotten that God wants to get you away from your old life, as far as possible. Most ladders that you see in the street have the bottom in the gutter, and that is where your ladder was originally. In God's sight the ladder you started to climb by faith was in the gutter. As long as you stay on the bottom rung you can put one foot down into the gutter again, can't you? This is the danger of staying at the bottom of the ladder – you can rest your feet down in the mud again. Have you forgotten that he wants to get you away from that? Up the ladder as far as possible from where you were before, and he wants you to travel. So don't forget that. Don't be short-sighted or forgetful, but get up the ladder to be increasingly effective and fruitful.

Another thing that happens as you go up is this: you make your calling and election sure. There is an amazing phrase, considering that your election is sure because God decided it.

God elected you, God called you. What does it mean "make it sure"? Once again it is perhaps necessary just to have a little bit of a Greek lesson. The tense of the verb or the voice of the verb is what's called the middle voice, which means that it is best translated this way: make sure for yourself your calling and election. It means that the higher you get up the ladder the surer you will be that you are on it. That is terribly important. God wants you to be sure.

Part of the assurance comes from the witness of the Spirit. But it also comes from the witness of your conscience, that we have behaved ourselves in a certain way in the world. That is an assurance that we need. The higher you go up the ladder the more confidence you can have and the more you prove to others that you are in the way of the Lord, and you can make it sure for yourself and for others by climbing up. Putting it in a simple phrase: progress is proof. If you are progressing in the Christian life, that is proof that you are a Christian – to yourself and to other people.

In the second half of v. 10 Peter talks about stumbling. We can think about slipping down a ladder. Ladders are dangerous things and Peter is anxious that there should be no slip. Keep climbing and then you are not so likely to fall. There is one thing about the Christian ladder that's different from all other ladders – the nearer the top you are the safer you are. It is easier to fall off the bottom than the top. That is a strange thing, isn't it? Peter's teaching is: press on, and then you're not likely to come to grief, stumble or fall.

We not only grow as believers, we usually do it under a leader. God in his wisdom and mercy provides those whose job it is to remind people that there is a ladder to climb. Peter says, "I know you've heard all this before and I know you've grasped it, but I'm going to go on saying it." I heard of a preacher who was invited three times to the same church to preach over a period of some two years. Each time he preached on the same text and gave the same sermon. It's the sort of nightmare that preachers have that they will do this once. Occasionally I think I have done it. At the end of the third time one of the deacons said to him, "We've had that sermon twice already." It was on "You must be born again". So the preacher said, "Well, have you been born again? I'll preach it again and again until you are." That was his reply, and you can make of that what you wish.

But a preacher's job is not to be novel. It is not his job to produce something new out of the hat Sunday by Sunday. It is his job to remind his hearers of the old things. It is the old, old story. A Bible preacher has nothing new to say that wasn't said two thousand years ago. It's one of the besetting temptations of the preacher, to strive after novelty, to try and find something that will tickle people's ears instead of reminding them of the old things. Peter says, "I'm going to go on reminding you." I find that I constantly need to be told about even simple things, and to be told again and again and again. Peter is going to do that. Jesus said to Peter: "establish your brethren". One way to do that is to go on reminding them of important things.

Not only did he intend to remind them while he was still alive, and he had been doing this for thirty years now, he intended them also to recall these things after he was dead. There has been much speculation as to how he intended to leave behind something which could be such a reminder. I think I know the answer, but I can only give it to you as my opinion. We know that Simon Peter not only wrote these two letters, but that he got hold of a young man called John Mark. He said, "Mark, I want you to write down everything I can remember to tell you about the life of Jesus." In Mark's Gospel we have Peter's memory of Jesus, his teaching and his way. It is in that Gospel that we have the most damaging stories about the character of Peter. Only Peter would give

Mark that. Here is this old man (for he must now have been about sixty) saying, "I'll see that after I'm gone you will remember all this." One way to do that is to write it down. Isn't it marvellous we have got the big fisherman's teaching right here in front of us now? We are being reminded of things that he was saying two thousand years ago.

One final point. The "ladder" not only enables you to enter heaven richly, the further you are up that ladder the better you can face death. Notice what a remarkable attitude toward dying Peter shows. This is Peter who was once so frightened of dying that he swore he didn't know Jesus rather than run the risk of being arrested and put to death with him. Peter now knows something that you and I do not know. I do not know how I am going to die. I have no idea. You are probably in the same position. You have no idea how you are going to die, whether it will be suddenly or slowly, whether it will be easy or a hard journey. But Peter did know because thirty years before Jesus told him how he was going to die.

Do you know what Jesus had said to Peter? "Peter, you will be crucified. You are going to be crucified." Those who had seen Jesus die on the cross had often seen the agony of people who were crucified – the horror of it, the loneliness of it, the pain of it, the suffering of it. Could you live for thirty years knowing that was how you were going to end? What a thought. Peter, who was getting older and frailer, knew that he was going to die that way.

Listen to him: "I know that I'm not much longer here. I know I'm going, the Lord Jesus told me." What does he say? He says, "It's just like pulling up my tent pegs." Isn't that a lovely phrase? He calls his body a tent. That is one way he talks. He also uses a word (in v. 15) to describe his departure which is used in the Old Testament and in the New. The word is "exodus". In the Old Testament the "exodus" was the first step towards the Promised Land. In the New

Testament the word occurs in one other place. It is in the account of the top of the mountain of transfiguration. Peter was there, and James and John, and Jesus. Jesus was standing between Moses and Elijah. Jesus, it says, was talking with them about his "exodus" in Jerusalem. A Christian thinks of death as a pulling up of the tent pegs and as an exodus that is going to lead into a Promised Land.

11

AUTHENTICATION

Read 2 Peter 1:16–21

Views of Bible:
      i. All true
      ii. All false
      iii. Part true, part false
      iv. Mythically and morally true,
            but historically and scientifically false

A. N.T. PREACHING (16–18)
     1. Not invented fables
        a. Power of Jesus
        b. Coming of Jesus
     2. But indisputable facts
        a. Eye-witness: saw the vision
        b. Ear-witness: heard the voice

B. O.T. PROPHESYING (20–21)
     1. Not human interpretation
        a. Insight
        b. Imagination
     2. But divine inspiration
        a. Communicated from God
        b. Carried by Holy Spirit

We are still looking at the second letter of Peter as a school for Christians. Christians need to go to school – that is the way we grow up and mature.

Now we are going to have a history lesson. There are two ways of learning history. One is to learn modern history by asking those who have witnessed it and been there what happened. But most of our history has to be learned out of books because the people who were there are no longer here and so we get it secondhand.

I remember how boring history seemed at school. As far as history goes I would share George Bernard Shaw's dictum that education begins the day you leave school. I understand what he meant, for I had no interest in history at school. It seemed to be the most boring subject – because it had nothing to do with me. What did it matter to me what Mary the Queen of Scots did, or Robert the Bruce, or Napoleon, or Julius Caesar? I've got to live now. Not until many years later did I realise that a study of history is a profound help to living now.

Someone has said that the punishment for not learning history is that you will have to relive it. There is something to be said for learning the lessons of the past. Certainly if a Christian does not learn history he will not grow – not the history of the world, not the history of Napoleon or Julius Caesar, but that section or chunk of history which is covered in the Bible. That section of history is concerned with one part of the world. The Bible is a book of history. It has the battles, the kings, dates and much else. At first sight it is as boring as any other history book. When you begin to realise why God wrote it down it begins to be the most exciting bit of history. Here it is. One of the things said in the Bible is: "Of making books there is no end, and much study is a weariness to the flesh."

There is another statement in scripture: "... if all the things that Jesus had said and done were written in books, the whole world would not be big enough as a library to contain the books." Fortunately, there is only one book that a Christian needs to study. If he reads others, and it is very helpful to do so, he reads them to help him to understand this and apply it in other realms. But we are people of a book and one book, and the Bible will always be the book of Christianity.

Mind you, there will be no Bibles in heaven. Peter tells us in this passage why we won't need Bibles in heaven but we do need them now. Nobody has any right to criticise the Bible until they have read it through. When anybody says to me, "The Bible's full of contradictions or difficulties," I say, "How much have you read? Have you read it right through?" "Well, not quite...." You find actually they have only dabbled in bits or got it secondhand.

The very first thing to do to someone who criticises the Bible is to say, "I don't think you ought to criticise it until you have read it, so go away and read it through." Christians should read it right through – many have never done so but I rejoice that more are doing this. You can do it by reading three chapters every day and five chapters every Sunday, which is not much. Don't gallop through it, take your time and think about it as you read. It is good to read the Bible through aloud. We did that, day and night, right through, in one church of which I was Pastor. It is good for people to come and sit and listen to all of God's Word, parts they have never heard before. It is not a gimmick. We want to tell them that we believe the *whole* Bible and we are going to read all of it to anybody who will come and listen. That idea is really catching on. It takes about four days and people say, "Isn't it just a novelty, a gimmick?" See what happens when people hear the whole sweep of God's Word.

What is the Bible all about? Is it a series of great lives? Is it simply a history book of a nation called Israel? Three things Peter says right at the beginning of this passage in 2 Peter tell you what the Bible is all about. First of all, it is about a person. It is about our Lord Jesus Christ. All of it? Yes, all of it. If you want a lovely book to read as well as the Bible, to help you understand and enjoy the Bible more, get a book by a Mrs Hodgkins entitled *Christ in All the Scriptures*. It has a chapter on every book in the Bible, from Genesis to Revelation. Each chapter tells you what that book says about our Lord Jesus Christ.

A man whose faith was saved by that book was a bishop in Pakistan. After three years theological training his brain was so filled with scholarship, so filled with critical questions, so filled with a variety of opinions, that when he read the Bible he was analysing it, criticising it, and doing everything with it but one thing – he wasn't reading it to find Jesus, and he was going to resign from the ministry. Then an old lady gave him *Christ in All the Scriptures*. It shook him to realise that the Old Testament is a book about Jesus. He had always thought if you wanted to know about Jesus you read Matthew, Mark, Luke, and John. So he went back to his Old Testament and he read it looking for Jesus, and he found Jesus in every book. That bishop (Shandhu Ray) became one of the most effective and famous Christians as a result. God saved his faith when he saw that the Bible is all about Jesus from beginning to end. If you read it without finding Jesus then you will miss the point.

Secondly, Peter says it is about the *coming* of Jesus. Everything builds up to that, and yet that coming is a double event, a double coming. He has been once and he is coming

179

again. The whole of the Bible may be said to be about the coming of Jesus – the first or the second part of his coming to our planet. The Old Testament builds up to his first coming, yet even in the Old Testament his second coming is promised. It is all preparing over those fourteen hundred years for a little baby in Bethlehem, and then he comes.

What is the New Testament about? It is all about leading up to his second coming. Three hundred times in the pages of the New Testament his return to this planet Earth is mentioned. So we could say that the subject of this book is all about the coming of Jesus. Furthermore, it is about his coming *in power*.

On his first coming he had the power to heal and forgive and to save. On his second coming he will have the power to conquer, and to resurrect all believers, and to banish Satan. It is a coming in power. Now this was the heart of the message of the apostles, Peter included. The Old Testament led up to his coming, the Gospels say he has come, and the epistles and Revelation say he is coming back. If you trace that thread through, you have got the key that unlocks the whole book.

Now I am going to deal with a question I am frequently asked: Is the Bible true? There is a variety of opinions on this. I give you just four opinions. Number one: the opinion that this book, all or most of it, is unreliable stuff, made up years after the events happened; it is a production of man's imagination. Voltaire, the French philosopher and scientist, felt like that. He said, "The Bible, it's just not true. You can't rely on it now. We know now that scientifically and historically it's not true." He predicted that a hundred years after he died you would only find this book in a museum— people would have realised that it was not true. His home in Paris where he said that, became the headquarters in France of the British and Foreign Bible Society, its rooms stacked with thousands of Bibles to the ceiling, going out to every part of the world – so much for Voltaire! People who say the Bible is just not true, that all or most of it is unreliable stuff written up so many years after the event that they didn't get their memories right, finish in their graves while the Bible goes on. I am not going to say any more about that view because I don't think there are many thinking people who will hold it.

A second, far more common view is that parts of the Bible are true and parts of the Bible are false. As soon as you hold that view you are into a problem: which parts? Like the curate's egg, the Bible is good in parts, they tell us. So what are we going to do about it? Their answer would be go to the scholars and the scholars will tell you which parts are true and which parts are not true. The only snag is that every scholar you go to has a different opinion on which bits are true and which are not. The more you go to, the more bewildered you get until you say, "Well, if they don't know which parts are true and which are false, then how can I know?"

A third view often expressed today is that the Bible is all true in one sense and all untrue in another. Now what does this view exactly say? Let me try to put it in simple language. This view says that this is a book not of fact but of myth – fables. It's a bit like Aesop's fables, stories that may have a truth in them, a "moral" that you can call true, but you mustn't ask if the event of the story actually happened. It is like saying, "All work and no play makes Jack a dull boy." Is that true or not? If you say, "Well, yes it's true; that is the sort of thing that happens in life", that is mythical truth. If you start saying, "Well who was Jack and what kind of work did he do and where did he live?" People will say, "There is no Jack, it is just a fable, a truth expressed in Jack's life," Jack being a mythical figure.

It has become very popular nowadays to say Moses was

a mythical figure; that Jonah was never swallowed by a fish – again, that is just a story to get across a truth; that there were no such people as Adam and Eve, there is just a moral in the story. As if all the Bible is a lot of fairy tales with morals – you will find that a very widespread view.

I heard of a little child talking about the vicar of the church. He used to tell little made up stories to the children to get a truth across, but he wasn't one of those who, having told the story, went on and on applying the moral at the end. This child was heard to say, "I like our vicar – he has no morals." She meant this kind of fairy tale with that endless moralising at the end. The Bible doesn't do that. The Bible just presents you with a true story and says, "There it is." It is not a book of fables.

A fourth view is that the Bible is a book of history – *his* story, a book of facts; it's a book of events, which actually occurred. One of the great delights of our day is that one science, of all the different sciences, has done more than any other to make people feel this is real – the science of archeology. In the last hundred years the science of archeology has really developed. They have been digging around in the sands of Egypt and the rubble of the Middle East and unearthed so much.

I think back to when I got the book *The Bible as History* by Werner Keller. At three o'clock in the morning my wife called down from the bedroom, "When are you coming to bed?" I said, "When I finish this book." It takes the unearthed discoveries of modern archeology and shows that at point after point the Bible was proved true.

Until the mid twentieth century, people said Pontius Pilate was a myth. For there was no record of his name anywhere in Roman history, no occurrence of the name anywhere but in the Bible. I remember the thrill when I stood at Caesarea on the coast of Israel on an archeological site with the diggers working all around, sifting the dust and looking at the stone they had discovered with "Pontius Pilatus" on it engraved in the granite, and they knew that Pilate was not a myth, he was real. Nebuchadnezzar was thought to be a myth and the book of Daniel a book of fairy tales, but now we know he was real.

This is the fourth view and it is a view that is being vindicated daily with discoveries. It is the view that the Bible is true, not only morally and spiritually, but historically. My faith is not based on fables with a moral, but on facts. Peter's faith was also based on facts. Do you know that within thirty years of Jesus' death, they were already saying Jesus was a myth? They were already saying, "It's a fairy tale, you've made it up." So Peter says, "We did not follow cleverly devised myths." We haven't given our minds to fairy tales. He says, "We saw and we heard." That is pretty strong evidence. No second hand evidence here. You see, God had been busy saying things and doing things for fourteen hundred years in the history of Israel. Peter says, "The things he said we heard, the things he did we saw." This was quite literal.

I was in a room in central London with a large number of theologians. I don't know how I got into it, but there they were from colleges all over the land. Somebody expressed an opinion (which they thought was acceptable to the rest of us) that the idea that God could talk was out. It was the "God is dead" idea, which was then current. They were all nodding agreement that God didn't talk. I said, "But I believe he does."

They looked around at this strange character! They said, "Well, you mean he gives ideas to people?"

"No," I said, "He speaks. He talks in such a way that you can actually hear him with these physical ears."

They said, "Well, what makes you think that?"

I replied, "On the top of the mountain of transfiguration God said, 'This is my beloved son in whom I'm well pleased,' and they heard it with their ears; they actually heard God talk."

On another occasion, God talked and the people thought it was thunder, but some heard the words. I wonder what you would feel like if God spoke now. It would sound like thunder. It might be so loud you don't catch the words but Peter caught them and he said, "We were on the holy mountain. We were there, we heard God talk." Myths? You believe your own ears. You believe your own eyes. "We saw his majesty."

It is quite clear that for Peter the most outstanding experience in the life of Jesus was the day they went up on top of a mountain and Jesus' clothes turned so bright. In colloquial language, Peter says, "You couldn't have got them brighter with any detergent on earth." You couldn't have washed his clothes whiter – they were shining out.

They saw two people who had been dead and gone for hundreds of years. *They saw and they heard* – that is not a myth. That was so real that Peter, writing thirty years later, says, "Do you think we'd follow fairy tales? Do you think we've invented all this? Do you think these are cunningly devised myths? We were on the mountain and we heard God speak and we remember the words that God said and we saw the glory of God in Jesus Christ." And so say all of them: the prophets of the Old Testament and the apostles of the New were those who said, "We saw; we heard."

There is no reason, except your own unbelief, for denying their evidence. There is no scientific reason, there is no historical reason for denying what they saw and heard and what they wrote down for our benefit. This, then, is my own understanding of the Bible. I don't believe that it is a mixture of bits that are true and bits that are false. I don't believe it is simply a string of fairy tales with morals – myths with morals. I accept the Bible's claim for itself, Peter's claim here, "What we heard and what we saw is what we based our faith upon."

Now let's move a little further than that. I'm going now into the Old Testament, for Peter does. He speaks of his own experience as an apostle, and every book in the New Testament rests on an apostolic experience and testimony – that is why they put these books together. For there were many other things written about Jesus. There have been many other "gospels" written. Some of them are full of myths. If I mention some of the stories to you that have been written about Jesus you would sense straight away how mythological they were. Let me give you one or two.

Two are called the "Gospel of Thomas" and the "Gospel of the Hebrews". We now know that the "Gospel of Thomas" was not written by Thomas and the "Gospel of the Hebrews" was not apostolic, but here are some of the stories. One is of Jesus as a little boy playing in Nazareth, and another little boy runs past and pushes him into the mud and Jesus stands up and curses the little boy with leprosy – that is one of the myths. Another is that Jesus as a boy made little birds of clay and blessed them, and they turned into real birds and flew away.

There have been many legends about Jesus, but just to tell you them I think you know there isn't the ring of truth in them. Why were we given the books of the New Testament? Because these are the books that have apostolic testimony behind them. Others wanted to cash in with false books. We live in an era when there is now commercial possibility in the name of Jesus, and his name is going to be exploited.

In the twentieth century we had plays on television like Dennis Potter's *Son of Man*, musicals like *Jesus Christ, Superstar*, and people cashing in with myths about Jesus.

The "Jesus" of *Jesus Christ, Superstar* is not the Jesus that they saw and the Jesus they heard. The "Jesus" of the musical got no further than the cross and never came out of the tomb. That is not the Jesus they saw and the Jesus they heard. For with their own eyes and their own ears they saw him after his resurrection, and that opera was simply exploiting the fact that Jesus was news.

In the early days of the church they had to select, they had to say, "That does not have apostolic testimony behind it – it is myth." It took them over a hundred years to get it all sorted out. They finally did so, and passed on to us the writings that the apostles lay behind, and now we have them. Says Peter: we did not build our faith on cunningly devised myths; we separated from that; we dealt with that; we were concerned with the truth. I do not believe there is a legend in this book, it is truth. But how did it come to be in the Old Testament? How could they write about Jesus hundreds of years before he was born? That is a big question and we must now look at it.

Before we do so may I just point out one little word at the end of v. 19 – "You will do well to pay attention to this as to a lamp shining in a dark place until the day dawns and the morning star rises in your hearts." What does all that mean? The psalmist in the Old Testament said, "Your word is a lamp unto my feet, a light on my path, it will show me where to go." The word translated "dark" can mean "dismal", "dirty", or "squalid". The Bible is like a little lamp in a squalid place. What a description! But what a privilege to be able to take a little lamp into a squalid place. It has been just that. Wherever the Bible has gone it has lightened up people's hearts. They have seen light here. But one day we won't need it any more. "When the day dawns and the morning star rises" – what is a morning star? It is a star so bright that it shines even when the sun is shining. The bright and morning star is a figure of speech applied to Jesus in this book, because one day Jesus will appear in the sky. The morning star is not the star that goes out when the dawn comes but the star that shines when the dawn comes. When Jesus appears you leave your Bible at home, you won't need it. You will see him and the dawn will come.

That was what it was for the Old Testament prophets. The Word of God was a lamp in a squalid place until Jesus came and then the light shone. There was a star – a morning star in the sky that was so bright that people could come a thousand miles to find a baby at Bethlehem. How shall a young man cleanse his way? By taking heed thereto according to your word, a lamp.

How did the prophets write things so long before they happened? How did the prophet David (for he was a prophet) write that the Messiah would die by having his hands and feet pierced? How was he able to write that they would gamble for his clothes and give him vinegar to drink? How could he write that a thousand years before it happened, when crucifixion was not even known and nobody had ever been put to death by having their hands and feet pierced? How were the prophets able to predict how history would unfold? How was it that they could predict exactly what would happen, and it did to the letter? How did they know Jesus would be born in Bethlehem? How did they know that the great city of Babylon would become ruins? How did they know that Nineveh would follow the same way, and Tyre and others? How did they know that at the end of history Israel would come back to her own land?

Peter says, "When you read the prophecies I want you to understand this..." [I will give you a free paraphrase to bring out the meaning:] "That no prophecy is a man's private opinion." No prophecy comes out of a human brain. It comes from the mind of God through a human mouth. Now that does not mean that God used people as typewriters and typed out his message, treated them as machines. The amazing thing to me is that if somebody says, "Is the Old Testament a human book or a divine book?" you get the same variety of opinions as we dealt with earlier. Some say, "It is purely a divine book, there's no trace of any human influence in it at all", but that doesn't seem to fit the facts. Some say, "It's purely a human book to be read like any other book, it's not a divine book." Others say, "There are patches that are human and patches that are divine," and then they go to arguing as to which is which. However, I believe that the Old Testament is human and divine, as is the New Testament – that when God the Holy Spirit takes a person he can use even their personality in such a way that the result is a perfect revelation of his word. That is real power – to be able to use fallible human beings to convey an infallible message of truth. That is what the Bible claims to be. I don't know if you have ever heard prophecy exercised, but when you do you know that is not that person speaking, it is God speaking, yet God is not treating that person as a machine but using them. So that their personality is not denied and not pushed out of the way but used to convey a message that is of God.

There has been over the last few years in England a revival of the gift of prophecy and it is a beautiful gift. People of God speak as the Spirit moves them. The word "moves" is the same word that is used in the Greek language for the wind blowing a ship along, carried along by the Spirit. How do you think they were able to talk about Jesus hundreds of years before he came? How could they write a book about Jesus in such clear terms that he was able to say, "Search the Old Testament"? For that is what he meant by "search the scriptures". No New Testament had yet been written, "Search the Old Testament, for it's all about me."

Well, Peter says, "Holy men of God spoke as they were

moved along by the Holy Spirit." That is how prophecy comes. It is not someone sitting down to think out a sermon. It is not someone with a great brain analysing history and seeing the trends and discerning where it is all going. It could be a very ordinary person. Amos was just a farm labourer. He said, "I was no priest, I was no prophet, I was just a farm labourer." And God said, "Go and speak." Amos said, "Thus says the Lord," and out it came. Amos's personality comes out too, and yet what came out was God's truth and God's Word. That is the lamp that we have.

Here is the most thrilling part. Every history book I ever had at school was all about the past. That is what made it so boring. It was all dead and gone, musty. It smelt of the cemetery, it was way back there. But here is a book of history that is about *all* of history, from the very beginning of history: "In the beginning God created the heavens and the earth," right through to the very last day of the history of our planet, "... and the earth and the heaven passed away and were no more." It is the only history book you have that is right the way through from the beginning to end.

Towards the end of his life, H.G. Wells decided to write the history of the world because he felt he had seen so much. Indeed, he did guess quite a bit of the future. Some of his science fiction is really quite up to date. He saw rockets, for example, but how little he saw. He put all his life into that book. He studied all the aeons of past history. He tried to start at the beginning because he wanted to warn people how it was all going to turn out, but he failed. It is a book that few people read nowadays. The Bible is the book that millions are reading. For holy men of God spoke as the Spirit of God moved them, and because what they said of Christ's first coming came true, then what they say of Christ's second coming will also come true. What they said of history that is now gone by, and came true, helps us to realise that what they have said about history yet to come will also be true.

Revival begins when people get into their Bibles and realise all that God is going to do, and realise that the prophets of the Old Testament and the apostles of the New together pointed up to the power and coming of our Lord Jesus Christ. He is coming again, and I give that to you on the authority of this lamp in a dark place, on the authority of this book. He is coming again to raise from the dead all who trust in him. He is coming again to establish a kingdom of righteousness and peace. He is coming again to abolish war. He is coming again to inaugurate the kingdom of God.

That is as certain as the fact that William the Conqueror came here in 1066. It is as certain as the fact that Julius Caesar invaded England in 44 BC and as certain as the fact that one day Jesus was born in Bethlehem of Judea.

Peter gave a history lesson we need if we are going to grow up – and you are going to have to realise that our testimony and the testimony of the prophets is not myth, not fairy tale, it is truth.

12

IMITATION

Read 2 Peter 2:1–22

A. THEIR DECEPTION (1–3)
    1. PERFORMANCE
        a. False prophets (O.T.)
        b. False teachers (N.T.)
    2. PREACHING
        a. Destructive heresies
        b. Denying Lord
    3. POPULARITY
        a. Many will follow
        b. Bring truth into disrepute
    4. PUNISHMENT
        a. Their greed
        b. Their condemnation

B. THEIR DESTRUCTION (4–10a)
    1. God can punish
        a. Angels
        b. Noah's society
        c. Sodom and Gomorrah
    2. God can preserve
        a. Noah
        b. Lot

C. THEIR DECADENCE (10b–16)
    1. Revile – angels
    2. Revel – animals

D. THEIR DANGER (17–22)
    1. Take people back
    2. Make people worse

We are treating the second letter of Peter as a school for Christians. In chapter 1 we went through three very simple lessons: Christian arithmetic (remember those mathematical signs); Christian gymnastics (remember the ladder that we are to climb), and Christian history, or reading, and the place that books and studying God's book have in growing in grace and in the knowledge of our Lord Jesus. Chapter 2 is not about lessons but about teachers.

In the Christian school you can choose your teachers and indeed have a responsibility to do so. There are two sorts of people who evade the responsibility of choosing their teachers in the Christian faith. The first are those who never *select* at all – those who simply accept anything they are told by somebody recognised in a church or denomination. For example, there are those, we could say within the Baptist denomination, who will accept anything a Baptist minister says because, after all, he is a Baptist. That is no selection at all. The opposite way is of those who never *settle*. Like butterflies in a flower bed they run from one teacher to another, they pick up a little bit here and a little bit there, and they lose out. Now in this chapter Peter is teaching: you are pupils in God's school; choose your teachers; choose the good ones, sit under them, and avoid the bad ones. For from the very beginning, where the truth of God has gone, the lies of Satan have very quickly followed. Wherever God's truth has been preached, Satan sends along a man to twist it and to pervert it. There are two ways that Satan attacks the church of Christ. One of them is dealt with in the first letter of Peter; the other is dealt with in the second letter. The first way is persecution from outside. The first letter of Peter is all about the sufferings that come when the church is attacked from outside. The other way the devil attacks the church, which is usually more effective, is by perversion within rather than persecution from without – by planting within the very church of Christ those who will take the Word of God and twist it and preach what is not God's truth. Invariably, as Peter says, it will be done in the name of liberation, in the name of freedom, in the name of liberal ideas. This "liberating" freedom, which is preached, is not liberty, it is slavery. That is Peter's point here and we are going to build up to that as we go through the chapter.

How does a false teacher twist the Word of God? Surely anybody getting up with a Bible in their hands and preaching it is going to preach the truth? I am afraid that is not true. Satan is too subtle for that. There are at least four ways I know of in which false teachers within the church take the Bible and twist it to the destruction of orthodox belief and orthodox behaviour.

I wish in a sense they would leave the Bible alone altogether and admit that they are not teaching it and teach their own ideas and see how many people they could get to listen. But when it is done with an air of preaching this Word and yet it is not, God's people are confused and bewildered. Here are the four ways I know. Number one: to *subtract* from the Word of God, to take things out of it and leave them alone. That is to take things away from it, to take a text out here, to take a passage out there, and even a book out there, and to snip it up with scissors, and to take things away from the Bible so that what you are left with is not the whole truth. Satan is too clever to tell us an outright lie – we would recognise it. What he does is tell us a half-truth. You have a perfect example of that in the Garden of Eden. He gave Adam and Eve a half-truth. He said, "When you eat of the fruit of the forbidden tree, your eyes will be opened", and that was true. But he didn't tell them what they would see. He told them they would be like God and that was not true. They ate, and their eyes were opened, but they didn't get to be like God.

The second way in which you can twist the Word of God is to *add* to it. Beware of anybody who knocks at your door or comes to you and says, "I believe the Bible and here's another book that we've produced to go with it which you must have also if you want the whole truth." Beware of that. The Bible alone is the only book that gives you the whole truth, and if anybody says you won't understand the Bible unless you have this book with it, which we have produced, beware. It is like putting luggage into a canoe. You can put so much in that it turns upside down. Don't add any other volume to your Bible.

A third way that false teachers distort the Bible is actually to *change* it. Beware of anybody who comes to you and says, "The Bible in your hand is not accurate, you need this one. You need our Bible. We have produced our translation." You will find that they have slipped in words that are not there in the Bible that you have. I will give you one example of that. One sect knocking at your door will try to sell you their translation of the Bible, which has altered John 1 very significantly. In my Bible and in yours it says, "In the beginning was the Word and the Word was with God and the Word was God." That is Jesus it is talking about—*the Word was God*. In their translation they will tell you that your Bible is wrong and that there should be a little word of one letter inserted in that verse and it alters the whole thing: In the beginning was the Word, and the Word was with God, and the Word was "a" god. Suddenly you are into a different idea and if you ask them, "Do you know if that word "a" is in the original?" they will freely admit that it isn't. They would be surprised that you knew it wasn't, and it isn't. That is a third way to change the Word of God.

The fourth way is to *ignore* it: to give out your text, and then ignore it and preach your own ideas. I have heard of one preacher's comment afterwards: if his text had had the measles, his sermon wouldn't have caught it! Now I know what is meant by that, and I heard of another preacher who said, "My text is so and so. I have two points tonight. Number one what is in this text and number two what is not in this text, and since I am short of time I'm going straight on to my second point." Well, at least he was honest. Yes you can ignore the Bible even while you quote it, and you can slip in your own ideas using the text as a pretext rather than in its context. I'll leave you with that sentence, puzzling it over, while I move on. All of this is tampering with the truth. Now why should anybody tamper with the truth? Why should people take the Bible and start messing it up? Why should they start adding to it and cutting bits out of it? Why should they start changing it and ignoring it? What motive can they have? Because bear in mind that Satan only uses those who are willing to be used. He doesn't force you to do things. He just attracts you to them and you must be willing to be a false teacher to be one.

There are teachers called of God – and by the way, if God hadn't called me I wouldn't dare to be one and I wouldn't want to be one. But when you are called of God there are pressures put upon you, subtle pressures to change the message – and I face them all so I know what they are. There are basically four which come, and here they are. Number one is the pressure of *intellectual pride*. It may interest you to know that just as there are fashions in dress and there is a pressure to keep up with the fashion in dress, there is also fashion in ideas. One of the pressures on ministers and preachers and teachers is to want to be up to date with ideas, to be able to preach the latest philosophy and the latest theology. It is a subtle pressure because you meet your fellow ministers and they are all quoting the latest philosophers and you have never heard of them. You think: "Oh, I must catch up. This is a thing to preach this year." Germany and central Europe have been the leaders of fashion in ideas and philosophy. It has been a subtle pressure to want to keep up with the latest German theological scholarship. To keep up with the fashion there is the subtle pressure to be modern in outlook, to change the Word of God so that people can say "How up to date he is, how thoroughly modern he is, right up to the minute."

The second pressure is *moral weakness*. For there are times when we teachers have to get up and say things that we know we have got to say to ourselves. We are faced with two possibilities: shall I go on preaching the high standards of God knowing that I don't live up to them, that I need God's grace, or shall I water it down and bring the sermon down to my standards so that then everybody is happy? That is a very strong pressure. Nobody likes to preach publicly beyond what they have achieved and I must preach a holiness that is beyond what I have achieved.

The third pressure is that of *social reputation*. I mean by that the desire to be popular. If you think preachers or teachers are the only ones to be afflicted with this, believe me it afflicts most of us: the desire to be well thought of by others.

There is no doubt about it that new ideas tickle people's fancy. In Athens there was a Mars Hill, a sort of Hyde Park Corner, where crowds gathered to hear some new thing, and provided you had a novel idea, a new approach, people came. Now a teacher of Christ is called to tell the old, old story over and over again. The subtle pressure is to try to say something new rather than something true, because that will tickle people's fancy. They won't say "We've heard it all before." People like to hear something new. That is why people who write scripts have nervous breakdowns. They have got to find something new. Tell a joke once on television and it's finished. You can never use it again. So they are trying to find something new all the time to keep people interested and entertained. Of course you could think that a congregation is there to be entertained and try and get something new, some new line, some new gimmick, some new dodge.

The fourth pressure is that of *material gain*. New ideas can be commercially profitable. It is profitable and always has been to give people exactly what they want.

Why do people become false teachers? Precisely for these reasons—they are mentioned here in 2 Peter 2, and there are pressures on your teacher and preacher that you need to pray hard about. They are there, for your preacher is human just as everybody else is. In the Old Testament, for every true prophet there was a false prophet. Every man who came with the truth, Satan saw there was another prophet alongside with the opposite. Think for example of the prophet Zedekiah – a false prophet who was deliberately put against a true prophet, Micaiah. When Micaiah was telling the people what God thought about them, Zedekiah was buttering them up, saying, "Don't listen to him, God thinks you're quite good." Or think of Jeremiah the true prophet, a lonely man, and he was plagued by false prophets by the dozen. In particular there was a man called Hananiah and whenever Jeremiah said, "God says it's war," Hananiah would come along and say, "No it isn't. It's peace. God won't let war come." Jeremiah paid for that with a lonely suffering. But he spoke the truth. In the New Testament we find that the same thing happens: whenever a true preacher comes along, a false teacher comes along afterwards. Wherever Paul went to set the Gentiles free to worship God, along came a false teacher and said to them, "You've got to become Jews and get circumcised." He was plagued by this and had to write letter after letter to deal with it. Jesus said that there will be wolves in and among the flock. Paul said the same when he said goodbye to the Christians in Ephesus. He said "Feed the flock" to the elders as he wept, as they said goodbye on the seashore, for he knew that after his departure, grievous wolves would get in among the flock with false ideas.

In vv. 1–3: *false teachers deceive*. They smuggle in the ideas secretly and suddenly you are aware that a false teaching is being given, something that is against the Word of God, and you think: "How did that happen – how could a person in that position be saying this kind of thing?" The answer is that it has been smuggled in over years; it is brought in secretly and suddenly there it is. What is their message? Their message is one of heresy. It is amazing how people have come to hate that word and to think it is wrong to hunt heresy. Why is that wrong, to hunt poison? If a policeman goes out with a dog trained to sniff out drugs, is that wrong? What does the word "heresy" mean? It is a very interesting Greek word and it means to choose for yourself. A heretic is someone who has chosen for himself what he believes. He has not listened to God. He says, "I've chosen what I believe." A heretic is a man who goes by his own thinking, not by God's; by his own arguments, not by God's; by his own ideas of what is true and not by what God has revealed. If we kept that meaning to the word "heresy" then I think we would rescue it from the rather nasty atmosphere it has got into. Heresy is any Christian choosing his or her ideas for himself or herself. This is smuggled in secretly, says Peter. The result is that such people deny the master who bought them. Remember who is writing this. Remember that one day Simon Peter denied the master. Here he is saying: you are going to do what I did. You will regret it as I did. You will weep bitterly afterwards as I did.

Notice the phrase "who bought them". The false teachers he is thinking of are those who say, "Now that you are a Christian you can do what you like. Now that you are a Christian you are free to do anything. Now that you are a Christian you are your own person." Instead, the true teacher says, "Now that you are a Christian you are not your own, you are bought with a price. You are not free to do anything you like. You are only free to do what *he* likes." That is the truth. The false teacher says, "He didn't buy you, he just set you free." No – he bought you, he paid for you, and therefore you are not free, only free to love and serve him.

Their *message* is that of heresy, their *manner* is that of licentiousness, which will have two effects, says Peter – one to attract many, and two to bring the way of truth into contempt. Increase the quantity but decrease the quality. That will be the effect of their manner.

Thirdly, their *motive* – what will it be? Says Peter: to desire more, to possess more, to exploit more, to have more money, to have more possessions, to get something from those they mislead, and their method (and here is a very interesting phrase) will be the use of plastic words (v. 3). We live in a world where people mould things to any shape. Plastic is something that is taken and just pushed into any shape you want. One of the things the false teacher does is to use words and mould them and push them into any shape he likes so that people think he's using the right words – and he is not, he is moulding them. It is what we call in modern language "double-talk". You say one thing and you mean another. You use the right word but you don't give it the right meaning. People use the word "Jesus" and they mould that word until it does not mean the Saviour and the Son of our God. Peter gives us a picture of their deception.

In vv. 4–10 Peter teaches that God can and will punish

those who have misled the flock of Christ and taught them wrong things. What will happen? The same has happened to the angels who fell; the same has happened to the society of Noah; the same happened to Sodom and Gomorrah. People who have taught wrong things will end the same way these did. The angels are being kept even now for punishment. Noah's society was obliterated so that there is no trace. Sodom and Gomorrah were so wiped out that the only thing left was a graveyard and they have only been able to find the Sodom cemetery and nothing more. God will punish – but having said that, Peter goes straight on to say don't worry, God can preserve. Out of the flood of Noah's day, eight people got out of it. Noah preached rightly. Out of Sodom there came a man with his wife and his wife didn't want to leave and she hung back and, according to the Bible, she was engulfed in a form of salt, buried alive, but Lot got out. We are told that Noah and Lot got out because they said: whatever anybody else is teaching, this is the truth and this is what is right.

We move on from their *destruction* to what I have called their *dissipation*. They are now compared with animals on one hand and angels on the other. Compared with the angels they revile more than angels dared to, and compared with animals they revelled more than animals dared to. This is strong language. I almost tremble to read it. The angels, even when they sin, still show some respect for God. But these false teachers will show no respect for the glorious ones. Animals? I do not know of an animal who has ever died from over-indulgence. But men can behave so much worse than animals that they are no better than the beasts born to be caught and killed.

So there is a comparison with all of the rest of God's creation: whether angels, they are worse than angels; whether animals, they are worse than animals. In fact Peter says there is a case in the Bible where an animal had more sense than a man. Do you know the story of the ass that spoke? You may not believe it but it is true, it happened. A donkey spoke more sense than a man. It happened one day when a man called Balaam, a good prophet, a man who spoke the truth of God, was told to go and speak to a nation and tell that nation that God would defeat them, and that nation didn't like that so the king offered the man called Balaam a lot of silver and gold if he would predict that God would give him victory. Balaam was reluctant to do so at first and then he went along. He got on his donkey and he settled the donkey and he trotted down a road between two walls. There came a point where the donkey just refused to go any further and the donkey was aware of the presence of an angel. (Sometimes animals can sense something more quickly than humans. A town in the United States slid down some wet clay and the town disappeared into a chasm. Do you know that for hours before it happened the dogs were barking and nobody knew why?) This dumb animal sensed that there was an angel of God in the middle of the road. It refused to go further and Balaam whipped it, for he was going to sell his soul to give false teaching. Finally, the donkey lay down. As Balaam whipped the donkey, the donkey spoke. God can put words into an ass that can bring a man up with a start – even the animals can show more sense than a man sometimes. This is the *dissipation* – reviling more than angels, revelling more than animals. That is what false teachers do.

Fourthly, in vv. 17–22, their *degradation*, shown in a series of horrible pictures. Peter gives us an image first of a waterless spring – what a contradiction! It means people will come thirsty and want a drink and they will go away parched. There is nothing to drink, nothing to refresh. There is another picture: a mist driven by the wind. So fleeting, so passing. The ideas of the false teacher will be gone in two years' time.

Philosophy will have moved on. The hungry sheep look up and are not fed. Here are two things a false teacher does: he sends people back to the life they came from when they came to Christ; and he puts them in a worse state, because having gone back to it they are twice as hard to win again. A false teacher, in the name of liberation and freedom, says now that you are a Christian you can do anything you like. Now that you are a Christian you can do again the things you did before you knew Christ. He is saying to a dog, "Go back to your own vomit." What a picture! The dog and the pig are the unclean animals in scripture. If a dog is sick, it is because there is something in its stomach that is bad for it, so it vomits it out. In the Middle East dogs are not kept as pets, they are scavengers – hungry, mangy brutes roaming the streets. One of the bad habits of the dog is that having vomited out something that is bad for it, that is disagreeing with it, you will find it going back later to lick it up again. A false teacher encourages that to happen.

Peter teaches us that it is better never to have come out of that, never to have got rid of it, than to come out of it to Christ and then teach people to go back into it in the name of liberal ideas and liberal thinking and liberal behaviour. That is the freedom Peter tells us is *not* to be taught. The freedom that we have in Christ is not freedom *to* sin but freedom *from* sin.

I am going to be very personal: not to you but to myself. Do you realise your responsibility to those who teach – to pray for them; to encourage them to preach the truth? Every time you resent being taught the truth of God and show it, you discourage that teacher from teaching the truth. I heard a lovely story of a new minister who, when he arrived his sermons were full of the latest theology and ideas but he didn't preach Christ. He didn't include the person of the Saviour, and one dear old lady left a little slip of paper on the pulpit for him: "They have taken away my Lord and I know not where they have laid him." It had little effect so a few Sundays later she put another slip of paper on the pulpit and she wrote on it a text that appears on a brass plate on the back of one pulpit from which I taught: "Sir, we would see Jesus." This had the desired effect and he got back to teaching the truth, so she put another slip of paper on the pulpit: "Then were the disciples glad when they saw the Lord." She was a wise old lady. She knew that she had a responsibility to her teacher to keep him teaching the truth, the whole truth, and nothing but the truth. So in a quiet way she kept him on the straight and narrow track. That is not an invitation for a pile of pieces of paper in pulpits!

Once a minister came to me, very discouraged and very disheartened. "What's the matter?" I asked. He replied, "There's a man in my congregation who does nothing but criticise my sermons. Every Tuesday morning there is a long letter telling me what was wrong with my sermon and it is just knocking me down and down." I mention that for balance!

Pray for your teachers and help them. If they begin teaching things that are going to damage the church of Christ, tell them in love: "that's not going to help us; get back to the truth." Any teacher worth his salt will get on his knees before the Lord and say, "Lord have I been giving way to these pressures and have I become a false teacher?" If that is true, either he must change or he must pray that God will take his congregation elsewhere.

Note

For comments on the surprising similarity between this chapter and the letter of Jude, see my commentary on that epistle.

13

COMPLETION

Read 2 Peter 3:1–18

INTRODUCTION (1–2)
       Peter's Letters:
           i. Reminiscence; wholesome thinking
           ii. Recall scriptures
                  Predicted by prophets (O.T.)
                  Promised by Jesus (N.T.)

A. WRONG REACTION – SCOFFING (3–7)
       1. Kind of people (3)
         a. Sceptical
         b. Self-indulgent
       2. Delay exaggerated (4)
         a. No coming
         b. Since creation!
       3. Destructive flood (5-7)
         a. Day of Judgment
         b. Ungodly men

B. RIGHT REACTION – SANCTIFIED (8–14)
       1. Delay explained (8–9)
         a. Time is relative
         b. Time for repentance
       2. Destructive fire (10, 12b–13)
         a. Old heaven and earth
         b. New heaven and earth
       3. Kind of people (11–12a, 14)
         a. Holy and godly
         b. Spotless and blameless

C. CONCLUSION (15–18)
       Paul's letters (15–16) a. Obscure; b. Distorted
       Peter's readers (17–18) a. Fall; b. Grow

The second letter of Peter might be subtitled "a school for Christians". We have been studying it from this point of view. In 2 Peter 1 we looked at the various lessons that Christians need to learn in the school for Christians. In chapter 2 we considered the teachers in the school for Christians. Chapter 3 tells us that one day school will end. I heard a lovely story of a little boy who was sent off to school at the age of five for his first day, and at four o'clock the teacher said, "You can go home now." He stared in disbelief and then he said, "My Dad said I was here for ten years!" When you are at school it seems to stretch ahead, homework seems eternal, and you think you will never get away from it. But one day school ends. At the end of school there is usually an examination. Therefore the more you think of the end of school, the more you will prepare for your finals.

A dear old lady in her eighties was sitting, reading her Bible. She was asked why she was reading it and she said, "I'm swotting for my finals." She knew that one day you leave school and there is an examination at the end of your school days. It was Keats the poet who called this life the vale of soul making. He meant that it is a school to prepare for a much larger world. If we forget the larger world then we won't make enough of the school. There will come a day, then, when school closes down – this world as we know it will disappear and we will have finished our time of learning. God will test us to see how much we have learned while we have been in the school for Christians. But how will school end? Ringing a bell? Well, a trumpet is going to sound.

But there is also a disaster that is going to end school. The school of this world is going to end tragically, disastrously, unexpectedly, and Peter is talking about this and telling us to be ready for the day the school goes. First of all he talks about the *promise*. The promise is that one day there will come the *day of the Lord*. That phrase occurs many times in the words of the Old Testament prophets and many times in the New Testament. What does it mean? It means that people have had their day and one day God is going to have his day. Other little men have had their day and cease to be but God's day has yet to come. God has never really had his day on this earth, and one day the day of the Lord will come and what he says will have to be obeyed. So the Bible looks forward to the day of the Lord, which may be much longer than a day of twenty-four hours – that is what a day is to me, but a day to the Lord is very different.

That "day" includes at least three events. Event number one will be *the coming of the Lord*. In the Old Testament they thought that meant Yahweh and they looked for the day that he would come. We now know about this more fully – we now know that the day of the Lord, when the Lord comes, is the day of *Jesus* coming. One thing is absolutely certain: that Jesus is going to step right back into this planet of ours. Are you ready to meet him? The coming of the Lord is the first event Peter mentions here. The second event he mentions, which is part of the coming day of the Lord, is *the end of the world*. That used to be scoffed at. In the nineteenth century, people said, "The end of the world? Ridiculous!" But since the two world wars of the twentieth century, people don't laugh at this idea any more. Some young people will tell you they doubt if they will live to die in their beds of old age. The end of the world is terribly real now, indeed even among people who are not Christians. There is a sense of things building up to some huge crisis, some great disaster.

They are right, too. Things are building up. You don't need to try to persuade people today that the end of the world could come, nor need you persuade them that it could happen in the way that Peter describes in this chapter, which we will come to later.

The third event, which he mentions as part of the day of the Lord, is something that nobody in the world even dreams could happen. Those who believe this world came by chance could not believe this third thing because statistically it just couldn't have happened again by chance. It is *a new heaven and a new earth*. A whole new universe with new space, new planets in it – and only the Christian knows about this one. So Peter talks about a new world. If you want to find the part of the Bible that talks about God's creation, read the first three pages and the last three pages. You will be astonished. It is like reading the same thing all over again. In the beginning *God created the heavens and the earth*. That is the first page. Read the second last page: *I saw a new heaven and a new earth for the old heaven and the old earth had passed away*.

So we have seen that there are three events about which Peter is teaching us. I want you to know that Jesus used the word "regeneration" of two different connections. He said to an *individual*: "You must be born again." Individuals must be regenerated, given a new life, made all over again. But he also used the word "regeneration" of the *universe*. Just as individuals need to be born again, so the universe is going to be born again. God is going to regenerate the whole thing. The people he is giving new life to are just the beginning of a new creation which will reach to the furthest limits of space. What a conception—the whole thing is going to be reborn; the whole thing is going to be regenerated. One day you will just see a big bonfire and a new universe arising from the ashes.

That, then, is the *promise*. We come, secondly, to what I

call the *prediction*, the crucial question: when is this going to happen? This year? Next year? Sometime? Never? There are three groups of people around: the fanatics who say "this year, next year"; the scoffers who say "never", and the believers who say "sometime". When I say "fanatics" I mean those who try to improve on God's Word and date the day of the Lord. It can't be done.

There are still some signs of the times that have not yet appeared. There are those who panic people. I remember hearing of some who led a group of people to climb a hill in Somerset and wait for the Lord's coming. Jesus said this sort of thing would be liable to happen. "Don't listen to them," he says. You will all know when it has really come if you are watching and praying. Don't listen to the fanatics who will give you dates. That is not the way to do it. But at the other end are those scoffers who say "Never, there's no sign of his coming; everything's continuing as usual – there is no sign whatever that there is going to be a climax to history. We'll be here for another million years and we'll just go on and on and on." They are guilty of the disease "euphoria".That is the disease of saying to yourself it can never happen. You hear of road accidents and you say "It could never happen to me." You see that the burglars have been in a house three doors away and you say "It could never happen to me." You hear of someone stricken with a disease that can't be cured and you say "It could never happen to me." But sometimes it does happen. What does Peter have to say to people like this?

First: *it has happened once so why shouldn't it happen again?* God has already once brought a whole era to an end. He has already once removed a whole society from the face of the earth. He did it with water then, but he did it and a whole society vanished. If he has done it once, why could he not do it twice? Peter got this argument from Jesus himself, because Jesus said, "As it was in the days of Noah so it will be in the days when the Son of Man comes again." Here is the second thing Peter teaches. Do you realise the first time God destroyed the world he did it with an element already in it – *water.* He didn't need to create anything new to do it. The water was there. It was there in the sky, it was there in the ocean. We are told two things happened in Noah's day. The rain came down in a cloudburst, and the land must have been so disturbed that it sank, because it says the waters of the oceans rushed in. The combination of the water from above and the water from below wiped out a whole society. The new element he is going to use is not water but *fire.* The fire is already there. He doesn't need to introduce anything new. It is only a few years since a scientist said that if we knew how to start the right kind of chain reaction, the whole universe would burn up in fire in forty minutes. If a scientist says that, then he is just catching up with God. God would not need to create anything new. Every atom is made up of energy that could dissolve in fire if we could release it, and God would just need to start the event.

Peter says that the same God who said he would destroy the earth by water has said he would destroy it by fire. You have the same word. One of the frightening things about the Bible is that God means what he says. Now here is the second group of scoffers who say "Oh it will never happen – it's all right, you can't go on forever; the world will always be there" – but it won't.

However, the true believer neither falls into the panic group who says "this year, next year" and starts getting all excited, nor does he fall into the scoffer category, saying "Oh, it will never happen in my lifetime." What he says is "It is going to happen sometime." It may seem slow, it may seem as if God is waiting an awfully long time, but there are three things at any rate that we need to remember.

Firstly: *time is different to God.* How God feels about the time since Jesus died – a couple of days. To God, who has been there always, a thousand years is just like breakfast to supper time. So to God it doesn't seem a long time. That is the first thing to get into your head. Two thousand years is only a couple of days to God.

Secondly, there is a reason why God is delaying this, a reason why he is keeping school open, a reason why he is keeping us in after time, for, in a sense, we wish he had closed down the school long before now. The reason is this: *he wants more people in his family*. He wants more people to repent and come to him. Every day God gives us is a day when something like twenty-five thousand more people find Christ, and God wants that. He doesn't want to destroy anyone.

Every day he gives you another day to repent. That is why he seems to us to be slow – it is his mercy. Thank God that he hasn't drawn the curtain before now on world history. We have an opportunity to come to God because he gave us another day.

The third reason is that even if apparently there are no signs of his coming, even if it doesn't seem like tomorrow, remember that his coming is like a thief in the night, and if you had known the burglar was coming you would have stayed awake, you would have watched. You would have sat up and waited for the first sign of his coming. So Peter says: "Watch". The Christian who is watching will not be caught out. A Christian who is awake and alert will hear, will see, will know that Christ is coming. It is only those who are asleep who will suddenly find the burglar has come. The day of the Lord will be upon them like a thief in the night.

What about the practice of all this – is it relevant to daily life? Some people say if you concentrate on the second coming and the future you are living "pie in the sky and then die when you die"; or, "you're heavenly-minded and no earthly use." Is that true? I don't think so. There are three things that will happen to someone who is looking for the day of the Lord. Firstly, he will *wait* for it. James says he will wait like a farmer waits for the harvest. You can't be impatient with the harvest. I farmed, I know. You can't keep going out and, when you see a bit of green, pull it up to see how the roots are doing and push it back in. When you have sown the corn you must wait patiently. A Christian doesn't get all panicky and excited about the second coming. But he waits patiently for it and he watches the sign of the harvest day coming. *Waiting* is the first reaction.

Secondly: *hastening the day*. There is some doubt about the translation here and I am not surprised by that. Some early copies of the New Testament have changed the word "hastening" to something else. I think they changed it because they found the idea just too difficult. Peter wrote "hastening the day of his coming". It was changed to "hastening towards the day of his coming; hasting to the day of his coming". Let us go back to what I believe Peter wrote. It is in my hands to hasten the day of the Lord. Here I am torn between two. I know that the longer it is the more people have a chance to repent, and yet you know I want to bring it nearer to get into that new heaven and earth.

How do I resolve this tension? By bringing in the lost ones. The more the church gets on with its job, winning the lost, the nearer that day can come. God has said that we must make disciples of all the nations. Then the end will come. He wants a family with every representation of race and clan and tribe. We are to get on with that and he will bring his day. So you can see why God is holding the day off in order that all nations might respond. It is within our power to bring that day nearer when there is going to be a new heaven and a new earth. What a motive to get on with evangelism. Bible translators emphasise this because they know they are hastening the day of his coming.

A Christian will *wait,* will *hasten* and, thirdly, will *prepare* for it. The exam is coming so you want to be ready. Those who emphasise the second coming properly and those who look forward to the future are those who will say, "Since all these things are thus to be dissolved, what manner of people ought we to be?" It has a direct effect on your daily living. Our church buildings will one day be demolished. Everybody will have gone off to meet the Lord. That could be your first trip to the holy land, and you will meet the Lord and look down on the Mount of Olives with him. What a hope!

I had an aunt who was always getting her "last" piece of furniture. She used to say, "That's my last stair carpet. I won't need another. I bought my last this and my last that." If everything on the earth is going to be dissolved in fire we must not be the kind of people whose hearts are getting attached to the things that will be burned up or we will be terribly upset and we will lose. Our hearts should be set with affection on the things that are above where Christ is, so that when the bonfire comes, nothing that we cherish goes.

What kind of people ought we to be? We ought to be the kind of people who will come out at the end of the school with honours in God's test. Peter says there are two ways in which you can get ready. Firstly: *all manner of holy living.* Secondly: *be at peace with one another.* Wouldn't it be terrible if the Lord came for his church and found the church members at odds with each other? Wouldn't we feel ashamed if we were just having a row with someone and Jesus stepped out of the clouds and there we were? So let us be at peace with one another, that he may be pleased when he comes. That is the *practice* of it.

Finally: we must *preach* this. The apostles did. Peter has some lovely remarks here about Paul's letters. He says they are a bit difficult to understand sometimes. People can twist them. But he tells us that he and Paul say the same thing. Never set over against each other the writers of the New Testament. They all say exactly the same thing. They all say Jesus is coming back. They all say that "school" will close. They all say the trumpet will sound. They all look forward to a new heaven and a new earth. They all have the same message.

I am quite sure somebody had come to Peter and said, "Paul doesn't say what you're saying," and he says, "Paul does." You are twisting his words if you don't see that there. Read all the apostles: read John, Peter, Paul, they all say the same thing. They all tell you what is going to happen in the future, so listen to them.

In conclusion, there are certain things a Christian must not change and there are certain things a Christian must change. First, his beliefs about the future. Peter warns against being carried away with the mistakes of those who say "Where is the promise of his coming?" Don't be upset or disturbed by those who twist the teachings of scripture, and by how much in the last hundred years the teaching of the Bible has been twisted about the last days, to prove this, that and the other. Don't be upset; don't be misled.

But the thing that ought to change is this: that *you should grow in grace and in the knowledge of our Lord Jesus*. That defines the limits. The Bible puts strict limits to your beliefs: inside apostolic beliefs. Peter, Paul and John, taught the same thing and we must not step outside the circle of their beliefs. That must not change, but within the circle we can grow up within the ideas. You grow in grace and in the knowledge of our Lord Jesus. That is more than a head knowledge, it is a heart knowledge, a personal relationship.

For more of David Pawson's teaching,
including DVDs and CDs, go to
www.davidpawson.com

FOR FREE DOWNLOADS
www.davidpawson.org

Lightning Source UK Ltd.
Milton Keynes UK
UKHW050217141119
353452UK00012BA/1053/P